PROCESS-ORIENTED GROUP THERAPY

PROCESS-ORIENTED GROUP THERAPY

For Men and Women
Sexually Abused
in Childhood

Carolyn Knight, Ph.D.

L**P** LEARNING PUBLICATIONS, INC.
Holmes Beach, Florida

ISBN 1-55691-123-8

Learning Publications, Inc.
5351 Gulf Drive
P.O. Box 1338
Holmes Beach, FL 34218-1338

Printing: 5 4 3 2 1   Year: 10 9 8 7 6

Printed in the United States of America.

To my clients, past and present, whose courage has been such a source of inspiration to me over the years.

Special thanks to my family for their unwavering love and support and to my colleagues, Esta Glazer-Semmel, Glenda McNeill, and Marcia Meyer, for their willingness to read and comment on earlier drafts of this manuscript.

CONTENTS

The Accuracy of Memories • **Disillusionment with the Group:** Carol Decides to Quit the Group • Anticipating Disillusionment • The Therapist's Support System • **Dissociation During the Session:** The Therapist Discovers Collective Dissociation • Monitoring Dissociation in the Group • **Discussing Sexuality:** Overcoming Shame • George's Confession • Connecting Childhood to Adult Behavior • Accepting Responsibility • Developing a Realistic View of Sexual Functioning • **Focusing on the Here and Now:** Bob Misunderstands Denise's Behavior • Conflicts and Disagreements • Members' Disappointment in Sally • Dealing with Connectedness • Members Reach Out to George • Group Self-Evaluation • Jennifer and Denise Comment on the Group's Resistance • Studies of the Here-and-Now in Group Therapy • **Frequent Laughter and Other Tension-Relieving Behavior** • **Resentment for the Therapist** • Dealing with Anger Toward the Therapist • The Therapist's Reaction to Anger

Denial of the Group's Ending: Sally Responds to the Therapist's Reminder • **Anger at the Therapist** • **Regression to Earlier Times** • **Increase in Expressions of Sadness** • **The Last Session:** Addressing an Unresolved Issue • The Difficulty of Ending

INTRODUCTION

This book grew from my eight years experience leading groups for adult survivors and discussing this work with colleagues. While there has been a veritable explosion of literature addressing the long-term consequences of child sexual abuse and describing groups for survivors, only a minimal amount of detailed discussion concerning group processes and therapeutic techniques has emerged.

In an attempt to fill this gap, the purpose of *Process-Oriented Group Therapy: For Men and Women Sexually Abused in Childhood* is to serve as a guide for clinicians either interested in or currently working with groups for adult survivors. In order to take some of the mystery out of group work with survivors, I have tried to provide a practical framework with the intention of making this intervention less threatening, and more manageable, understandable, and available to practitioners. I have not attempted to reinvent the wheel but generally have relied upon accepted principles of group treatment.

Readers who are familiar with the group-therapy literature will see quickly that I have relied upon the work of Irving Yalom, *The Theory and Practice of Group Psychotherapy*, and Lawrence Shulman's discussion of groups in *The Skills of Helping Individuals, Families, and Groups.** As a strong believer in the value of empirically based practice, I encourage clinicians to rely on the research findings and, whenever possible, on practice methods and techniques already found to be effective. While I have endeavored to provide readers with some background research, this book is, first and foremost, a guide for practice. Excellent reviews of research on groups

---

*Note: See *Selected Bibliography* on pages 169-181 for these and other books.

already exist. I have only highlighted and summarized research findings on selected topics I believe to be the most crucial and central to my work with clients. It made the most sense to me to include this information in an abbreviated, referenced format. The *Selected Bibliography* should provide a comparable context where the usefulness and relevance of these guidelines may be determined.

There are no tried-and-true rules about how to run a group for survivors. As more research is conducted in this area, therapists will have at their disposal more information concerning what works. Flexibility, responsiveness to member feedback, and the therapist's personal preferences should all play an important role in decisions regarding group structure.

My own working knowledge of survivors' groups continues to evolve. Eight years ago, for example, I began leading 12-week groups for women, where out-of-group contact between members was strongly discouraged. Based on feedback from group members, advice from colleagues, information available, and experience, groups now have been extended to 20 weeks, contain both men and women, and, while I still don't encourage out-of-group contact, I don't as strongly discourage it, either. Meanwhile I have seen how the powerful and intense experience of group therapy can address and correct the effects of childhood sexual abuse for survivors.

In **Chapter 1,** the long-term consequences of sexual exploitation in childhood are summarized and the rationale for the use of a mixed-sex group with adult survivors explained. The group experience provides survivors with numerous therapeutic advantages, providing strength, support, validation, and much-needed acceptance. In a group that includes both men and women, members also have the opportunity to talk honestly about sexuality, confront deep-seated and intense feelings of rage and sadness, and work on their feelings about and relationships with the opposite sex.

For those who are able to handle the demands, leading a survivors' group for adults is a rewarding and extraordinarily therapeutic experience. **Chapter 2** explores the role and function of the group therapist. In order for the therapeutic potential of a survivors' group to be realized, the therapist must have a clear sense of role as well as an understanding of how group treatment benefits its members. Chapter 2 identifies and discusses six separate but related tasks critical to effectively running a group for survivors, including convening the group and creating a group culture, integral tasks associated with any form of group psychotherapy. Given the unique treatment needs of survivors and the demands placed on the therapist, use of self and consulting with colleagues are also covered.

The therapist creates and structures the group as well as carefully chooses the members who will function within a group dynamic. **Chapter 3** provides an extensive discussion of group structure, guidelines for selecting members, and the pregroup interview. The pregroup interview provides the therapist with an initial determination of a survivor's capability of handling the intense, at times, overwhelming impact of the therapy group, their ability to make the necessary commitment and adhere to the required norms of the group. The therapist also uses the pregroup interview to explain the nature, demands, value and purpose of the group. Considerations for group size, time limits, group duration, session length, group goals and norms are also covered.

Group dynamics and appropriate therapeutic techniques in the beginning, middle, and ending phases of the group are discussed in **Chapters 4, 5,** and **6,** respectively. The dynamics of the middle, work phase of a survivors' group and the ability of the group to work effectively depend heavily upon the work accomplished in the early sessions. Issues emerging in the middle phase build upon and grow out of the earliest group themes. Even though the most dramatic work of the group takes place during the middle phase, some of the hardest work occurs in the beginning, as well as in the last session.

Chapter 4 covers the significant themes and issues that emerge in the first sessions as the group evolves, and members are just beginning to feel comfortable with one another. **Chapter 5** describes group dynamics evident in the middle phase of the group's life and reflect the hard work that is taking place. A prominent theme is the expression and management of powerful feelings of rage and loss. This helps explain at least two other dynamics — members' dissociation and wanting to quit. Group members continue to work right up to the last session. While members' work has been difficult and painful from the beginning, the group has provided a safe place with reassurance, support, and hope. **Chapter 6** covers how the therapist prepares members for the very difficult task of the group's termination.

I urge the reader to use my recommendations judiciously, cautiously, and only as a guide. I have described what I do and why. In addition to the rationale and research I have set forth in this book, I must add that what I do just "feels right" to me. To be sure, feedback from my clients reinforces this assessment, and much of what I have discussed is consistent with accepted practice wisdom, and the results of research on groups, generally. The challenge to each of us is to develop a style of interacting with clients that is consistent with our personalities, appropriate for the particular client, and likely to effect positive change.

I have tried to use case examples that are not only instructive, but provide readers with a true sense of what it is like for survivors in the highly charged, intense atmosphere that exists in therapy groups. The names of group members have been changed in order to protect the privacy of the individuals and their stories. The language and descriptions of survivors' victimization experiences are, at times, graphic. My intention is not to shock the reader, but to convey clearly and accurately what it means to work with adults who have been victimized sexually. I believe I would have provided a disservice to my clients and to all those clinicians who work with survivors if I had whitewashed or glossed over the pain and anguish that is so much a part of the therapy.

While working with an adult group of child sexual abuse victims is not easy, it is rewarding and gratifying work. My life, both personally and professionally, has been immeasurably enhanced and enriched through the relationships with my clients. I am grateful to have had the opportunity to assist survivors reclaim their lives, and I look forward to many more years of learning and growing with them.

1
Advantages of Group Treatment for Adult Survivors of Child Sexual Abuse

A group therapy experience has the potential to counter and correct some of the most debilitating and damaging long-term effects of child sexual abuse. While adult survivors of childhood sexual abuse share consistent emotional patterns of difficulties associated with self, others, and the abuse, and childhoods filled with trauma and pain, survivors also demonstrate common characteristics such as resiliency and inner strength — powerful motivators for positive change.

Long-Term Consequences of Child Sexual Abuse

Research questions are becoming more refined. Many early studies on the long-term effects of child sexual abuse focused on small, clinical samples of women. More recent investigations include men and women using non-clinical samples, controls, and more rigorous research techniques. While earlier works sought to simply identify the long-term effects of childhood sexual abuse, researchers now consider whether differences in the abuse itself and various family dynamics lead to different long-term consequences or whether men and women are affected differently by their sexual victimization.*

The term "child sexual abuse" is defined as sexual contact between a child and an individual in a position of power and authority. In this book this inclusive term refers to the childhood sexual victimization experienced by adult survivors and does not restrict the abuse to the family, as does the term "incest." Further, this term includes the full range of sexual activities in which survivors may have been forced to participate, including, but not limited to, fondling, masturbation, intercourse, or oral and anal sex. This definition also reflects the role that power plays in the sexual victimization of children. The perpetrator, who may or may not be an adult, is someone with authority and power, who exploits the child sexually. The perpetrator's use of power may or may not involve overtly coercive measures. Whether openly aggressive or subtly persuasive, a critical dimension of the sexually abusive relationship is the child's powerlessness in relation to the perpetrator. Perpetrators include parents, stepparents, family members, babysitters, teachers, and others.

Despite suffering a traumatic and painful childhood, adult survivors display resourcefulness, strength, and the potential for growth capitalized upon in treatment. The term "survivor" connotes the magnitude of the trauma experienced by the individual in childhood, a reflection of what Lawrence Shulman calls the "strength for change" (Shulman 1992). Survivors possess the ability to change their situation, and the therapist's

---

*For a complete discussion of the long-term effects of childhood sexual abuse, the reader is advised to consult any of the following: Alter-Reid et al. 1986; Briere and Runtz 1988; Briere et al. 1988; Edwards and Donaldson 1989; Feinauer 1988; Feinauer 1989; Finkelhor 1990; Finkelhor and Browne 1985; Freeman-Longo 1986; Fromuth and Burkhart 1989; Gordon 1990; Greenwald and Leitenberg 1990; Hunter 1991; Kiser et al. 1991; Mackey et al. 1991; Myers 1989; Palmer et al. 1990; Putnam et al. 1986; Salter 1995; Stein et al. 1988; Vander Mey 1988; Young et al. 1991.

primary responsibility is to build upon their clients' inner and external resources.

Survivors' Common Reactions to their Abuse

The most common long-term reactions among survivors are their feelings of responsibility for their victimization and the resulting guilt. Perpetrators often assign blame to their child victims and insist on secrecy, intensifying the survivor's sense of responsibility. Even when this is not part of the victimization, survivors often feel responsible for their abuse. This sense of responsibility also allows survivors to feel they have some control over their lives and protects them from frightening reactions associated with the abuse, such as intense feelings of rage and loss. Guilt serves a protective function: As long as survivors believe they caused the abuse, they can avoid the painful realization that persons to whom they looked for nurturing and security either did not protect them or sexually exploited them.

Fear and anxiety, two other common reactions to the sexual abuse, are emotional windows through which survivors perceive the world around them. Whether the survivor was injured or subjected to threats of injury to self or others if the abuse was disclosed, fear and anxiety in connection to discovery are common initial and long-term reactions to the abuse. As adults, survivors continue to view their social world with suspicion, sometimes bordering on paranoia. There is some evidence to suggest that when the sexual victimization is accompanied by threats or actual harm, and when the perpetrator is someone well-known and trusted by the child, the survivor is even more likely to experience chronic feelings of anxiety and fear.

Intense feelings of rage and loss also are common reactions to the abuse among adult survivors. Survivors experience a deep sense of sadness and anguish over the loss of childhood innocence, and the sense of self. Survivors harbor intense rage at those who exploited them and those who did not protect them.

Rage and loss are two of the most powerful and frightening reactions experienced by survivors, often denied and repressed. These feelings are problematic for both men and women but may manifest differently. Women appear to have an easier time acknowledging feelings of sadness, while male survivors are better able to connect with feelings of anger. While depression is a common characteristic for female survivors, evidence suggests male survivors, particularly, have problems with aggression. Survivors' problems with depression or aggression may be linked to manifestations of deep-seated and powerful feelings of rage and loss.

PSTD and MPD

In recent years, many authors have discussed the effects of child sexual abuse in terms of Post-Traumatic Stress Disorder (PTSD). Feelings, attitudes, and behaviors attributed to adult survivors are seen as traumatic effects of the sexual abuse. Besides common reactions already mentioned, many survivors suffer from problems such as flashbacks, full or partial memory loss, sleep disturbances, feelings of numbness, anxiety, and panic attacks.

Studies have been limited almost exclusively to female, hospitalized patients. Much less attention has been directed at determining whether PTSD symptoms are common among nonclinical, nonhospitalized survivors, especially among males. The PTSD conceptualization has been criticized on several grounds. One vocal critic, David Finkelhor, notes that it is too narrow and many survivors have problems that would not be characterized as reflecting PTSD. Finkelhor also argues that many survivors' experiences of sexual abuse are not consistent with the definition of a traumatic event. Several studies support Finkelhor's reservations regarding the relevance of PTSD for adult survivors.

Others have pointed to the relationship between child sexual abuse and dissociative disorders, most notably Multiple Personality Disorder (MPD). Dissociative disorders reflect child and adult survivors' attempts to deal with the abuse, and the resultant overwhelming feelings of shame, guilt, self-loathing, and fear. In the extreme, the survivor experiences the abuse as having happened to someone else. Other manifestations of dissociation constitute partial or complete memory loss regarding the abuse and suppression of affect.

Similar to PTSD, much MPD research has focused on clinical samples of women. Results consistently show that patients with MPD are more likely than those with other psychiatric disorders to have a history of childhood sexual abuse. At least one study using a nonclinical sample of college women found that dissociative symptoms also were more common among subjects reporting a history of child sexual abuse (Briere and Runtz 1985).

The Accuracy of Memory

Much debate in recent years regards the accuracy and veracity of survivors' recovered memories. Some critics argue that clients' supposed memories of sexual abuse actually are the creation of therapists with a priori assumptions about the existence of sexual abuse in their clients' histories (Mayer 1995). Skepticism is particularly strong regarding memories of events occurring before age three, given the child's cognitive immaturity (Terr 1990) and memories retrieved through hypnotic techniques (American Medical Association 1985). Some research evidence indicates that false memories in children and adults are most likely to occur around less significant issues or result from suggestions of close family members. (Loftus 1993; Ceci and Bruck 1993). In contrast, a growing body of research using clinical and nonclinical adult samples demonstrates that full or partial amnesia regarding the sexual abuse is a common reaction among adult survivors (Briere and Conte 1993; Herman and Schatzow 1987; Feldman-Summers and Pope 1994). The results of one follow-up study are particularly enlightening. The researcher interviewed 129 individuals who, as children had been treated in an emergency room for sexual abuse 17 years earlier. Nearly one-half of the subjects had or continued to have amnesia about their abuse (Williams 1992).

Feelings about Self

Survivors tend to suffer from chronic feelings of low self-esteem and inadequacy. Sexual abuse leaves the victim feeling bad, shameful, and dirty, which become permanent self-defining descriptors. Suzanne Sgroi has called this the "damaged goods syndrome" (1982). Pervasive feelings of inadequacy are presumed to be linked to the child's powerlessness at the hands of the perpetrator. Recent research suggests that chronic feelings of low self-esteem and inadequacy affect both men and women.

Chronic or episodic depression is another characteristic symptom of survivors that reflects chronic low self-esteem, self-blame, and intense feelings of inadequacy. Not only are suicidal thoughts common, but survivors are assumed to be at risk for suicide attempts. With suicidal ideation, this also appears to reflect the survivor's desire to escape or to end the pain, confusion, and unhappiness.

A growing number of studies have shown that survivors who experienced incestuous abuse, as well as relatively long-term abuse that involved more invasive kinds of sexual contact, are more likely to experience depression, low self-esteem, and suicidal thoughts. In one study aimed at differentiating effects of abuse based on race, results indicated that African-American women are particularly likely to suffer from these problems, owing at least in part to a more serious nature of abuse (Russell et al. 1988).

A connection between sexual abuse in childhood and later abuse of alcohol and drugs, particularly for men, has also been established. More recently, research connecting abuse and eating disorders in women also has appeared. While the precise link between substance abuse, eating disorders, and sexual abuse remains unclear, several explanations have been proposed. Many survivors come from alcoholic families. Their own substance abuse problems may reflect learned behavior and a genetic predisposition. Alcohol and drug abuse provides the survivor with a means of escaping pain and sadness. Eating disorders reflect survivors' ambivalence about their sexuality and self-hatred. Eating disorders also may reflect survivors' struggle with overwhelming feelings of powerlessness.

Survivors' Relationships

Survivors' isolation and deep-seated mistrust of others are well documented. Adult survivors feel they are different — they have a dark, secret side they feel they must hide from others. Their sense of betrayal regarding the abuse makes survivors extremely suspicious of others. With sexual abuse continually viewed as a woman's problem and therapeutic services traditionally geared toward women, isolation may be heightened in male survivors.

Survivors' relationships tend to be unhealthy, with the survivor being at particular risk of further victimization physically, sexually, and emotionally. The child feels powerless because of the abuse, and this leads to a diminished sense of self-efficacy in the adult survivor. Survivors' feelings of worthlessness contribute to their inability to exert appropriate control in adult social relationships.

Recent research suggests problems in adult relationships are particularly acute for survivors who experienced incestuous abuse that was of relatively long duration involving intercourse and other invasive sexual acts. On the other hand, at least one study of female survivors found that women who received support from nonabusing parents and others when they disclosed the abuse exhibited less impairment in their social relationships with men than women who had no such support (Wyatt and Mickey 1987).

Several authors have speculated that male survivors' fears about their masculinity and concerns about their sexual orientation, coupled with strong feelings of inadequacy and low self-esteem, may lead them to identify with the aggressor. While they are presumed to be at risk of victimizing and exploiting others, empirical support for the existence of such a relationship is inconclusive. There is some evidence to suggest that, compared with women, men are generally more prone toward hostile behavior because of their sexual abuse. Several studies of men convicted of a variety of nonsexual crimes show they are more likely than nonoffenders to have a history of sexual abuse.

Sexual dysfunction is a common problem among adult survivors. Sexual problems range from diminished or nonexistent sex drive, guilt, anxiety, orgasmic dysfunction, and confusion over sexual orientation to promiscuity and prostitution.

As greater attention focuses on the problems of male survivors, some authors have proposed that their problems with sex and sexuality may be particularly acute due to heightened concerns about their sexual orientation and adequacy. These two concerns may in part explain why males who were sexually abused in childhood are presumed to be more likely to become perpetrators.

While most male survivors are not likely to molest children, sexual abuse in childhood, coupled with a variety of not yet completely understood factors, places the adult male survivor at risk of offending. At least two studies provide support for this assumption. Urquiza and Crowley (1983), using a nonclinical sample of college students, found that men who had been sexually abused in childhood were more likely to report sexual fantasies involving children and a desire to fondle children than were all female subjects and men who had not been sexually abused. Mary Fromuth and her colleagues surveyed male college students and found that, among the small percentage of subjects who reported activity that met their criterion for sexual molestation of a younger child, the rate of sexual victimization in childhood was much higher than among the nonmolesters (1991).

THE ADVANTAGES OF THEME-ORIENTED GROUP TREATMENT FOR ADULT SURVIVORS

Given the difficulties with which survivors struggle, a group experience is a particularly appropriate form of treatment. Many advantages of group therapy for survivors discussed below reflect Irving Yalom's ideas on the curative factors of group psychotherapy (1985). Other benefits derive from the unique value of a therapy group containing both men and women.

Groups for adult survivors labeled in the literature typically as "support" groups, are for women only, time limited, and operated with an agenda developed and flexibly followed by the leaders.* Recently, the term "theme oriented" has been applied to groups such as the one described in this book (Drum 1990). A basic feature of theme-oriented group therapy is the underlying commonality of members' experience. While individual histories vary widely, all members of the survivors' group share a fundamental reality: They were sexually exploited in childhood or adolescence. This common bond is a driving force in the therapy group and underlies all of the important dynamics.

This underlying commonality among members clearly distinguishes theme-oriented group therapy from others. In traditional psychotherapy groups, heterogeneity with respect to presenting problems and life experiences is preferred. In theme-oriented therapy groups, membership is restricted to individuals with similar problems and life experiences. A theme-oriented therapy group for adult survivors is heavily dependent upon the professional leadership and judgment of the therapist. In contrast to self-help and many support groups that focus on members' "there-and-then" concerns related to the abuse, the theme-oriented group therapist also concentrates on their immediate, here-and-now interactions with one another.

In the type of therapy group described in this book, members do not run the group, nor do they serve as leaders, as often happens in self-help groups. Further, membership in the theme-oriented therapy group is not open nor is the group open-ended, two important features of self-help groups. Based upon the survivor's individual needs and considerations related to the group as a whole, the therapist determines whether a survivor is able to participate. Finally, the therapy group is open to both male and female survivors.

---

*See, for example: Cole and Barney 1987; Kelly-Garnett 1989; McEvoy and Minuk 1990; Sgroi 1989; Axelroth 1991; Apolinsky and Wilcoxon 1991.

Universality

One of the more powerful forces for change in a group is what Yalom has labeled "universality." Research findings suggest this factor is particularly important in short-term groups. Adult survivors' tendency to blame themselves for the abuse and their resulting feelings of self-loathing lead them not only to isolate themselves, but also to believe that they "are the only ones." Survivors are often convinced they are crazy due to their repressed or overt feelings of rage, despair, and fear, or problems with sexual dysfunction, memory loss, and eating disorders. The group gives members the opportunity to meet and connect with others, a phenomenon Shulman has labeled "all in the same boat."

As members discover they are not alone and their experiences, feelings, and problems are shared by others in the group, they are freed from worrying that they are different and can begin to concentrate on the work of changing. Members' common bond serves as a potent source of validation and affirmation. Since many survivors never disclosed their abuse or were met with disbelief, denial, or blame if they did, this is particularly important.

In the first session of the group, members are asked to disclose as much as they can about themselves and the circumstances surrounding their abuse (detailed in Chapter 4). Initially this produces anxiety for members, but it facilitates the rapid development of universality, that sense of not being alone. For many members, this comes as an "aha" experience.

Tom's Introduction

One group consisted of eight individuals, with an equal number of men and women. All four women and one man, Tom, had been in group and individual therapy previously; the other three men hadn't. During the first session, several members of the group had already introduced themselves and had provided superficial descriptions of themselves and their abuse.

When it was Tom's turn, he provided members with a detailed description of what had happened to him, and became increasingly angry and tearful as he did so. Tom, a 36-year-old recovering alcoholic, had been sodomized by his alcoholic father. He had been in individual and group therapy for some time, and was making significant progress. Tom ended his introduction by discussing his recently discovered rage at his mother, who, he was convinced, knew of the abuse but had done nothing to prevent it out of fear of her husband. His final comments were, "I'm feeling crazy . . . out of it. I've always put her on a pedestal. I thought she was a victim just like me. Now, I see she was just weak, with no guts, a lying, spineless bitch. She let that bastard abuse me. I hate her. She was a victim, so I feel sorry for her, too. But mostly I hate her."

While some initial discomfort followed these disclosures, it was quickly followed by an animated discussion among several members acknowledging similar feelings toward family members who had not protected them. One man said, "I can't believe this. Your tears are my tears, your anger is my anger. I never knew other men felt the same way I did. I thought maybe I should just have enjoyed the abuse, since I was a guy."

One woman commented, "I can't believe you're crying. I never thought men could cry. I have so much pain in me, but so do you. I've always hated my mother for what she did, but was always told by my brothers and sisters that I was cold hearted."

Tom's disclosure set the tone for the remainder of the group session. Several other members also revealed particularly painful experiences. In each case, they were met with validation, support, and the general mood as this first session ended was one of enormous relief by the members.

It is only when members reveal what they consider to be their darker, secret sides that the full impact of this group dynamic can be felt. On their own, members typically avoid discussing these issues. It is usually up to the therapist to help survivors share their secrets. While most visible as members are getting acquainted with one another, universality continues to be a powerful force for change throughout the group as members begin to trust each other, and become more willing to take risks.

Altruism

Members not only get help from others, they provide it in the form of advice, suggestions, comfort, and support. Because child sexual abuse survivors are plagued by feelings of worthlessness, low self-esteem, and inadequacy, being helpful to someone else boosts their sense of self-worth. Given the importance of this variable, the therapist must create an environment where members look to each other for validation and support. Members should be encouraged to share their suggestions and advice. The therapist might share her opinion and thoughts, but usually only after members have heard from each other.

Imparting Information

A related advantage of a group experience consists of advice and suggestions. The value of this therapeutic factor does not mean that the primary purpose of the group is didactic, nor that the main source of advice and insights should be from the therapist. Inevitably, members share advice and insights with one another. Given the importance of the process associated with this dynamic — the offering of advice sends a message about concern and caring — it is important that members be the primary sources of information.

While survivors have unique histories of sexual exploitation, they often experience remarkably similar problems and concerns. Shared insights are often helpful, instructive, and on target. Survivors often provide very helpful and much-needed guidance to each other.

Denise Identifies Sally's Concern

Sally complained to the group one night that her husband was "driving her crazy" with the way he was handling her daughter. Specifically, he would tickle and roughhouse with his two-and-a-half year old until she cried, ignoring the child's requests for him to stop. Members initially responded with advice about how to get him to stop and assurances that her concern was founded.

Denise, who frequently raises concerns and self-doubts about the handling of her four children, responded, "I think you're right to be concerned, but I know for me, when I get upset about stuff like that, it usually means that my buttons have been pushed. Do you think that maybe some of your anger at your husband is about the abuse, about being violated, and not being able to control your body? Like your daughter can't control her body because her daddy won't respect her right to say no?"

Denise's comments pinpointed the real issue. The predominate discussion in the group then focused on how members' rage and pain surfaces, often when they least expect it. Sally's concern reflected her strong sense of inadequacy. She wondered if she was right to think her husband's actions were inappropriate, or was she simply overreacting? With the group's help, Sally began to see how her husband's actions triggered in her deep-seated and chronic feelings of anger and self-doubt.

Instilling Hope

The power of the group to instill in its members a sense of optimism regarding their futures is an important factor since many have been struggling for years to cope with their experiences and its effects. Members, who are at different stages in the healing process, have the opportunity to witness the growth of others and appreciate their own development. Men and women just beginning therapy are encouraged and heartened by the progress evidenced by other group members who have been working on their abuse issues for some time. Members who have been in therapy for a while can compare their progress to others in the group. The value of diversity in the group underscores members' years and progress in therapy.

When survivors are dealing with particularly painful, difficult issues and question whether it's worth it or not, the group members provide each other with the courage and strength to keep going. Expressions of encouragement coming from other survivors are far more persuasive and meaningful than those provided by the therapist, since she or he is only a witness to the pain and struggle, not a participant.

Group Cohesiveness

The group comes to take on many characteristics of a family. Group members typically come from highly dysfunctional and unsatisfactory relationships in their families of origin. Even if their families were not the source of the abuse, they were unable to stop or prevent it. More than individual therapy, the group affords members the chance to work through problematic relationships with significant others.

The recreation-of-family dynamic may manifest itself in many ways within the group. One of the more common is members' jealousy and resentment of each other in relation to the therapist's attentions. This sibling-rivalry type of dynamic emerges from the inadequate, dysfunctional parenting experienced by most survivors. When members see how their past dysfunctional relationships influence and obstruct their current relationships they can begin to correct this problem.

The group affords members the opportunity to be intimate with each other and to feel connected, experiences that are often new to them. A sense of cohesiveness is one of the most powerful and unique advantages of group therapy. Given their tendency toward self-imposed isolation and low self-esteem, the paramount value of the group lies in its potential to boost members' feelings of self-worth. When survivors are truthful about their experiences and their feelings, and present themselves honestly to others, they are met with understanding and acceptance. Survivors typically have few, if any, opportunities to be intimate with others; they do not know what it means to experience acceptance and understanding in close relationships. The group provides them with a place where, often for the first time, they feel accepted, cared about, and important.

Jeff Describes the Group as Family

In the last session of a 16-week group, Jeff cried as he talked about what the group meant to him. During the group, Jeff had talked freely about his abuse and his feelings about his mother, father, and himself. Jeff's father, who had sodomized him, was also physically abusive, had intercourse with women and forced Jeff to do the same. Throughout the group, Jeff had freely expressed his anger and his pain, serving as an important catalyst for the rest of the group. As Jeff said goodbye, he commented, "You have all been like a family. No, you have been my family. I feel more connected here, more real, than I have ever felt anywhere, ever."

An underlying sense of connectedness to others and mutual acceptance inevitably leads to members' caring about and liking each other. With survivors, these feelings may be as problematic and intimidating as anger. Caring about others is threatening because it places the survivor at risk of being rejected. Being cared about by others is equally foreign and frightening. Survivors often question the motives and sincerity of others. Common concerns are voiced in questions such as, "How could they possibly like me?" or "What do they want from me?" A group experiencing cohesiveness and mutuality helps members accept the care and concern of others, as well as to express their own feelings of affection and regard for others.

Conflicts and Cohesiveness in the Group

While a cohesive group fosters a sense of acceptance and well-being among its members, it also encourages confrontation and conflict. Only when members feel comfortable and are honest with each other can they express their anger — what survivors perceive to be particularly risky behavior.

Research suggests group members have a great deal of difficulty providing negative feedback to each other. Survivors, particularly, are reluctant to express negative feelings. As children, many were punished when they expressed anger, or were targets for their parents' and others' hostility. Angry feelings in their present lives frequently trigger survivors' deep-seated rage concerning the abuse, often leading to spontaneous displays of rage. A group characterized by a sense of mutuality and cohesiveness allows members to experiment with expressing the frightening, but inevitable, emotion of anger.

The sources of conflict in a survivors' group are myriad. One primary dynamic underlying members' anger at each other is their distorted perceptions of each other, stemming from their histories of exploitation and abuse. Concern for each other is another dynamic that emerges as individuals in the group come to care about each other and become angry when a member does something that is not in his or her own best interest.

Susan Expresses Concern for Ben

Ben, a 42-year-old divorced father of two children revealed to the group that he had been frequenting gay bars that cater to individuals who like sadomasochistic sex. He had allowed himself to be "picked up" by several men and, in the sexual encounters that followed, he had been injured because of their actions. Initial comments from members reflected concern and fear for Ben's safety. Ben responded by saying that whenever he started to feel depressed or bad about himself, he felt like going to one of the bars "and getting screwed."

Susan angrily commented, "Why the hell do you want to do that to yourself? That's crazy. You're crazy." Susan's outburst was uncharacteristic, and the therapist asked if Susan was really expressing worry for Ben, but feeling unsure how best to help him. After thinking about this, Susan agreed, saying she "really liked" Ben, but was angry, mostly at his abusers, that he would take out his unhappiness on himself.

Members' anger at one another also reflects the inevitable difference of opinion and perspective that occurs in any intimate relationship. Relationships established within the group are like any others; the challenge in any intimate relationship is acknowledging and working through disagreements that surface.

Interpersonal Learning

One's sense of self and self-worth is intimately tied to the reactions and opinions of others. The developing child's sense of self is heavily dependent upon the responses of parents and other primary caregivers. When children are nurtured and receive messages of love, affirmation, and validation, they develop positive feelings of self-regard. On the other hand, parental rejection and hostility foster self-doubt and low self-esteem. In subsequent relationships, the individual's basic sense of self-worth is reinforced and confirmed. This dynamic is particularly troublesome for individuals who question their worth.

An important advantage of a group experience for survivors lies in its potential to interrupt the self-perpetuating nature of low self-esteem. The group becomes a social microcosm, the member's social world in miniature. Survivors' distorted perceptions of themselves and others can be challenged and deliberately worked on in the group. Members become more aware of their own behavior and their expectations of others, as well as how these influence the manner in which others respond to them. This awareness is essential before change in maladaptive relationships can occur.

Kevin's Story

When Kevin was 12, his parents were killed in a car crash, and he and his six siblings were quickly sent to live with relatives. Within two months of his going to live with a maternal aunt and uncle, Kevin was sexually abused by his uncle. The abuse continued for six years, becoming progressively more violent and sadistic, and involved several other adult perpetrators. Kevin ran away at age 18, supporting himself by becoming a male prostitute. When he found himself attracted to his 12-year-old nephew, he contacted a therapist and began group therapy.

Kevin typically presented himself as aloof and uncaring. He often ridiculed the comments of others, and tended to defuse emotionally charged situations by telling jokes and shifting the focus. Pointing these patterns out and suggesting he had to keep people at a distance to protect himself, the therapist explained to Kevin that he was setting himself up for the others to get angry with him. Initially, Kevin dismissed these comments as "ridiculous."

In the seventh session, Kevin told a joke after Mary had revealed a particularly painful aspect of her abuse. Once again the therapist confronted Kevin suggesting he was uncomfortable with Mary's revelation. Mary commented, too. "I'm sick of your jokes," she said. "Why are you here? All you do is make fun of others. What makes you so perfect?"

Kevin was visibly shaken by Mary's reaction and her tears. He never wanted to hurt her, he said, he "just had a real hard time opening up to others. I've kept this stuff in so long. I'm afraid of you. I don't know how to relate to people at all."

Kevin struggled with intense feelings of self-disgust and loathing. He had described his real, true self as "monstrous, gross, and disgusting." Expecting others to see him as he saw himself, he kept them at a safe distance by being rejecting, hostile, and condescending. While Kevin's behavior did not change overnight, without feedback from the therapist and members of the group, it is unlikely that Kevin's behavior would ever have changed.

Working on Relationships with the Opposite Sex

A group that includes both men and women truly represents the real world of survivors' social relationships. It affords members even greater opportunities to work on relationship issues than those in a same-sex group.

Some of the most problematic aspects of survivors' relationships involve feelings and behavior toward the opposite sex. Regardless of the perpetrator, survivors have deep concerns and reservations about the opposite sex. They approach these individuals with a mixture of fear, confusion, and, often, hostility.

In general, male survivors are afraid their sexual inadequacies will be found out by women, and female survivors worry that they will be hurt and exploited by men. Male survivors struggle with strong feelings of inadequacy and question their masculinity. Consequently, they are afraid of women, often defending themselves through generalized feelings of suspicion, mistrust, and resentment. Female survivors often harbor intense feelings of rage toward men and are frightened by them.

In a single-sex group, social-relationship problems can only be addressed in the abstract, if at all. It is only when men and women are both present that the anger, hostility, and suspicion that characterize members' relationships with the opposite sex surface, can be identified, and worked on. The dynamics associated with this phenomenon are some of the most powerful and therapeutic in the group.

Jennifer Faces Her Anger toward Men

In the fourth session of the group, several men had been talking about their relationships with women — the difficulty of having a lasting relationship and the fear of being used by a woman. Jennifer, who was becoming increasingly agitated, finally said, "I'm sick of hearing you talk about women. Women as users? Right! Men are nothing but users and abusers. I've never met a man who wasn't a user, starting with my father and his brothers."

Jennifer was somewhat surprised by her own outburst, saying that her anger "came out of nowhere." With some assistance she admitted, "I never knew how much I hated and feared men until I came to this group. Ever since we started, I've been pissed off at all of the guys here. I just wait for a reason to get angry."

Jennifer had worked on many aspects of the abuse itself. She had been in therapy for some time and had previously been in two all-women's groups. When she entered the mixed group, Jennifer was able to see how her anger and fear of men got in the way, distorted her perceptions, and consequently, her ability to relate to men. Jennifer was sexually abused by her father and his two brothers over a period of years; she also had been in other subsequent physically, sexually, and psychologically abusive relationships. It was only in a group containing men that Jennifer could begin to break the self-perpetuating cycle of exploitation, anger, and self-hatred that had governed her relationships.

Confronting Gender-Based Stereotypes

Survivors' understanding and expectations regarding the opposite sex are based upon rigid stereotypes and narrow definitions of what it means to be male and female. These expectations reflect survivors' own experiences as well as broader sociocultural values regarding appropriate male and female behavior. Female survivors typically believe, to a greater or lesser extent, that "all men are bad and out to hurt others" and male survivors feel "all women are vulnerable, weak, and manipulative." These stereotypes allow survivors to feel some measure of control over their social world by rendering the behavior of men and women predictable. This reflects the commonly cited phenomenon called "splitting," which is the tendency for survivors to view situations as either/or.

Group membership with men and women forces participants to confront these stereotypes and assists them in viewing themselves and others more realistically. Members' gender-based expectations are quickly challenged and disputed as they observe others behaving in individual and nonstereotypical ways. A group that includes both men and women not only allows members to confront their anger and suspicion about the opposite sex, it also affords them the opportunity to feel connected and comfortable with these individuals. As members honestly discuss their victimization and resulting feelings of rage and despair, a sense of connectedness between them is fostered. For survivors, long accustomed to isolation and estrangement in their relationships with the opposite sex, this is extraordinarily rewarding, enlightening, and therapeutic.

The longer members are together, the more they can be expected to talk freely and honestly about their gender and expectations for themselves and others. This discussion typically moves beyond merely focusing on the impact of members' abuse, and may be more accurately characterized as men and women attempting to come to grips with the ways they have been socialized to view themselves and others based on gender.

Concern has been expressed about the possible disadvantages for women who participate in mixed-sex groups. It has been argued that women may be more likely to assume roles in the group that reinforce dependence and subservience to men. Women have been found to talk less, talk primarily to the men, share less personal information, and to be less involved in the discussion when men are present in a group.*

The way members interact with one another depends to a large extent upon the therapist's expectations and actions. If she or he follows gender-based expectations for members, it is likely that their interactions with one another will reflect this. The therapist's own gender and his or her behavior also will strongly influence how members relate to one another. The therapist bears the responsibility for the expectations that members hold for themselves and each other. The therapist has the obligation to create an environment conducive to working. This demands that both women and men be encouraged to abandon traditional ways of behaving and managing distress.

While it is possible that women could be ill-served by being in a group with men, this does not have to be the case. A mixed group can be an important place for both men and women to work through their difficulties, as long as the therapist is sensitive to the risks involved and free of gender-based biases in her or his work.

Open Discussion of Sexuality

Perhaps the most difficult and embarrassing but one of the most important subjects for survivors to discuss openly and honestly is their sexuality. The presence of both men and women is a catalyst for focusing on sex and sexuality. Members

---

*See, for example: Lazerson 1992; Burden and Gottleib 1987; Beasley and Childers 1985; Carlock and Martin 1977; Reed 1981; Aries 1976.

are able to reveal some of their more embarrassing sexual secrets. These revelations sometimes reflect particularly humiliating aspects of the abuse. In other instances, they may entail survivors' sexual experiences as adults.

Examples of Group Members' Sexual Secrets

Denise revealed to the group that she has never been orgasmic with a man although she can achieve orgasm with her female partner. She refuses to let herself go, she told the group, to "give a man the upper hand." She has had an ongoing and long-standing lesbian relationship, but she wonders whether she is a lesbian, and has been afraid to admit to herself that maybe she is.

Mike told the group that he can't have normal sex. The only time he can have sex is if it's "kinky — the more anonymous the sex, the better." Mike said that he often lets himself be humiliated and degraded when he has sex, and doesn't understand it. Further, with great difficulty, Mike admitted that whenever he has tried to be sexually intimate with a woman whom he cares about, he "can't get it up."

June reported that "sex is her greatest weapon" and she uses it to get what she wants. June says that she doesn't really like it, and generally "takes off for parts unknown" when she's having sex. She is quick to point out that she feels like "a whore," and sometimes does accept money and gifts in exchange for sex.

Disclosures such as these can be expected to stimulate intense, frank discussions of members' sex lives. This provides further reassurance to members that they are not alone; their problems are shared by others. Not only does it help members to develop a more realistic and mature outlook toward sex, but members are able to become more accepting of their own sexuality.

Frank discussions of sexuality can only take place if the therapist is comfortable. It is incumbent upon the therapist to examine his or her own views about sexuality. Survivors are only too ready to avoid these discussions, though these ultimately lead to an enormous sense of relief. Thus, the therapist has the responsibility of creating an environment in which honest discussion of sex can take place and for encouraging members to risk engaging in such a discussion.

While seductive behavior is assumed to be common among survivors, reflecting their arrested sexual development, views of themselves and others as sexual objects, and attempts to control others, group members' interactions are generally free of seductiveness. The therapist should be sensitive and prepared to address manifestations of this behavior in group, particularly in discussions focusing on sex.

Members' ability to relate appropriately to one another in group may stem from their ability to completely suppress sexual feelings and may be another example of splitting. Interactions within the group may reflect a tendency to separate emotional intimacy from sexual intimacy. Members experience an emotional closeness that lacks any sexual content.

Survivors, both male and female, have a real need to talk about their sex lives and their accompanying feelings of guilt, confusion, and anxiety. Thus, when the opportunity for such discussion exists, members can be expected to seize upon it and make full use of it.

Managing Anger and Loss

A mixed-sex group has the potential to provide all participants with a forum for expressing difficult and overwhelming feelings. Female members typically have an easier time expressing their sadness. As they grieve about lost innocence and lost sense of self and self-worth, they are modeling appropriate behavior for the males. Men, whose anger is usually more apparent, voice the unspoken sentiments of female participants. Members' expressions of rage and loss provide other group members with a means of vicariously experiencing their own feelings and encourages them to openly vent their own feelings of anger and sadness.

This is not an easy task for survivors, who often expend a great deal of energy denying and suppressing these emotions because of the overwhelming intensity. The group therapist's skill in helping members acknowledge and express their feelings is critical. This also requires that the physical environment be conducive to controlled expressions of rage and loss.

Jeff Explores His Anger

For several sessions, Jeff had broached the subject of his anger toward his father for his abuse. Though encouraged, Jeff refused to explore these feelings further, claiming it was "too scary." In the eighth session, Jeff entered group already angry. He had been cited for disciplinary action at work and felt this was unwarranted. Again, Jeff was encouraged to vent his anger and the therapist noted that his anger about work was "similar to his anger over his abuse and the unfairness of it all."

Jeff said, "This is it. I'm going to explode." At that point, Jeff began pounding his fists on the carpeted floor and on the padded door, crying all the while. Other members of the group sat quietly, looking nervous and scared.

About five minutes later, Jeff returned to his seat and apologized for his outburst. Reassuring Jeff that apologies weren't necessary, that his angry outburst was necessary and inevitable, the therapist checked with other members of the group to see how they were feeling. The most common reaction was gratefulness to Jeff for expressing his emotions so honestly. Susan, who was typically quiet and withdrawn, said that she was "with him all the way. When he was hitting the door, I imagined it was my brothers' faces."

Several members said they were afraid, not of Jeff hurting them or even himself, but of his anger because of the proximity to their own rage. Carol remarked, "When I watched him getting so angry, I had to tune out, turn away. I know I have these feelings, but I'm so afraid of them."

Jeff's outburst was the first true spontaneous, raw expression of rage this group had experienced. While it was difficult for them, the members got through it. This was an important lesson: they could survive the painful process of recovery. In subsequent sessions, other individuals were able to spontaneously vent similar painful and intense feelings, crediting Jeff with giving them the courage to do so.

2

The Role of the Group Therapist

The therapist is critical to the effectiveness of a survivors' group. The therapist must recognize she or he has two sets of clients: Each individual in the group and the group as a whole. The therapist has to be centrally concerned with the well-being of the group, viewing the group as a separate and distinct entity. For therapists accustomed to individual therapy with survivors, this perspective may be difficult to appreciate and translate into appropriate behavior.

Confusion regarding the therapist's proper role and function may stem from a misunderstanding of the nature and value of support provided by an adult survivors' therapy group. The pain and despair of survivors may be so intense and overwhelming that the therapist may create a group atmosphere that is only superficially helpful.

Fran's Story

After attending several meetings with a woman's support group, Fran expressed her confusion, anger, and "disgust" regarding her experience. Fran identified two aspects of the group's functioning that bothered her. First, at the end of each session, members were required to identify something positive about themselves and their lives, and to think of something they could do in the coming week to "stroke themselves." Second, Fran reported that every time she tried to bring up "real feelings," such as her anger, the subject was "immediately" and "conveniently" switched to something else.

At some level, Fran knew that a group should be a place to talk about her feelings, and she was angry that such discussion was not encouraged. The group culture made her fear her feelings were wrong and abnormal. While the two leaders in Fran's group never stated a policy to not discuss intense feelings, their actions spoke louder than words. It was abundantly clear to all members that discussion of real issues was not allowed. To these leaders the group's purpose may have been to make its members feel good. The group environment may have reflected the leaders' anxieties about addressing members' intense feelings.

Fran's story underscores the unique and powerful role of support in a therapeutic group experience. It does not mean quick fixes and empty reassurances. What it does mean is an environment where members are free to discuss their deepest concerns, where such discussion is met with understanding and acceptance.

CONVENING THE GROUP

The therapist creates the group, and assumes sole responsibility for decisions regarding composition, structure, and norms of the group. Not all survivors are capable of handling the intense, emotionally charged nature of a therapy group. To place someone in an intense group atmosphere before they can handle it would be counterproductive and possibly harmful.

When convening the therapy group, the therapist also must pay attention to how a potential member's unique history, gender, and other personal and behavioral characteristics mesh with the rest of the group. This reflects the therapist's concern with the group-as-client.

The therapist must make informed and sometimes difficult decisions regarding who should join. The group therapist who is uncomfortable with this responsibility jeopardizes the group's viability and its therapeutic potential before it even begins. It is, therefore, important for the therapist to accept and use the authority and power inherent in this task, not shy away from it. The therapist needs the courage to restrict membership, if that is in the best interest of the individual, the group, or both. Such action, necessary as it is, does not come easily. Therapists must trust their judgment and expertise, even if they experience some ambivalence about their actions.

The Therapist Decides against Sheila

For a new group, the therapist interviewed interested individuals. She had received three self-referrals through the local chapter of the self-help group for adult survivors and determined two of the three women were appropriate. Sheila, however, who was extremely needy and fragile, was not ready for the rigors of the group. It was not an easy decision and was compounded by the fact that Sheila interacted with the other two women who were accepted for group membership. While an attempt was made to secure an alternative form of therapy for her, the therapist realized that no matter what she said or did, Sheila would feel rejected, hurt, and angry.

When the group started, the therapist raised the issue with the two female members who were acquainted with Sheila. Both women acknowledged they were angry, upset, and felt guilty that they had been accepted and Sheila had not, and expressed concern that they might be kicked out if they did anything wrong. While the therapist could say little about why Sheila had not joined the group, she did explain her rationale for the selection of members, validated Denise's and Sally's anger toward the therapist for hurting their friend, and addressed their unfounded, but understandable, fears that they could be asked to leave the group.

Such decisions are particularly difficult since survivors' pain and despair are so apparent. However, group membership decisions are crucial to the establishment of an environment where members can grow and change. Initially, it is only the group therapist who is in a position to know what is in the best interest of both the individual client and the group as a whole.

CREATION OF A GROUP AND DEVELOPMENT OF GROUP CULTURE

When members first come together, they are not a group; they are a collection of individuals. With the assistance and support of the therapist, they become a group. Whether this group becomes an effective agent of change is largely dependent upon the therapist's skill. The group therapist has two major tasks: To create a group out of a cluster of individuals, and to develop and maintain a group culture that promotes change and growth.

Developing Group Cohesiveness

The early sessions are critical for both tasks. When members first come together, they do not know each other, they only know the group therapist. The initial common, unifying force is not the members' shared histories of abuse, since these are unknown, but a shared acquaintanceship with the therapist, which provides the leader with a great deal of power. The skillful group therapist is the one who uses this position to develop a sense of "we-ness" among the members.

While members know they share common experiences, they remain estranged from each other. The group experience is new and strange, and like most people, survivors approach this situation with a mixture of fear and anxiety. Survivors, more than others, are reluctant to reveal their true feelings and true selves to others. While members' trust in the group therapist may not be high, it is higher than it is with the others in the group.

The first step in developing a sense of cohesiveness is for the therapist to foster interactions among members. Beginning in the first session, the therapist helps members share their histories with each other. While anxiety producing, introductions serve the valuable purpose of highlighting quickly and dramatically members' underlying similarities. Whenever possible, individual member's revelations should be used to point out the commonality among all members.

Jennifer's Risk-Taking Introduction

In the first session of one group containing four men and four women, names were exchanged and group rules were reviewed. Then the therapist asked members to introduce themselves. The first four members provided superficial histories, glossing over or avoiding painful and difficult aspects of their abuse.

When it was Jennifer's turn, she described in detail her abuse as well as her problems with alcohol, abusive husbands, and the molestation of her own daughter. As she talked, she became tearful, and had to stop several times to regain her composure. When she finished, there was an anxious, tense silence.

The therapist thanked Jennifer for her honesty, acknowledging how difficult this was for her to be so honest so soon. Jennifer was not alone in her pain, the therapist told the group. Others shared her deep feelings of sadness, and it was hard to hear these feelings articulated. The therapist turned to several members who were teary-eyed, asking them for their reactions, noting that Jennifer's comments seemed to have hit them pretty hard.

Lucy, who had already introduced herself, commented, "This is so hard. I try not to feel this stuff, but then I hear someone like Jennifer, and it all comes welling up inside me."

Joe agreed. "I'm new at this," he said. "I was warned it would be tough, but I can see that this is going to be the toughest thing I've ever done. I know how you feel, Jennifer. I feel that way, too."

Jennifer's comments sparked the beginning recognition of commonality among members. While a therapist might be tempted to empathize with and console a member such as Jennifer, such actions do little to develop group cohesiveness. The group therapist needs to capitalize on an individual member's sense of urgency and begin to build a sense of mutuality among all.

There are usually several members like Jennifer who can express a great deal early. In Jennifer's case, she had been in individual therapy for several years, had prior experience in an all-female group, and an accurate sense of the issues she needed to work on. As this first session ended, she said, "I was just waiting for someone to get things going, and since no one else volunteered, I figured, why not me?"

Much of the group therapist's efforts in the early sessions are directed at assisting members in seeing their commonality. Background knowledge of individual members is particularly helpful to the therapist in helping members to relate to each other. From the beginning, members should be discouraged from relying on the therapist and encouraged to reach out each other.

In the above example, as Jennifer discussed her abuse, she looked at the therapist. The therapist, however, was careful not to look too frequently at Jennifer, instead concentrating on the other members' reactions. Through this monitoring of the group the therapist was able to observe several other group members crying. By avoiding eye contact with Jennifer, the therapist encouraged her to reach out to others in the group.

Establishing a Group Culture that Promotes Growth

The ground rules for members' participation should foster an atmosphere in which members experience a sense of universality, acceptance, altruism, and cohesiveness; are free to discuss their secrets and deepest feelings of rage and pain; and begin to relate more effectively and comfortably with people of the same and opposite sex. Therapists' expectations for themselves and for the members' behavior must reflect these considerations.

The therapist's role involves not only establishing group norms that foster change, it also includes maintaining and strengthening the group's culture over time. The therapist's importance is nowhere more apparent than in the group's adherence to the norm of honesty. Without honest discussion, there can be no sense of universality, mutuality, or sense of acceptance and connectedness to others — in short, no real work will be accomplished. Open discussion among survivors does not come easily. It is not enough for the therapist to expect members to be honest with one another. The therapist must demand it.

Most survivors have spent a lifetime suppressing real feelings and hiding from others. If left to their own devices in group, the most difficult yet most significant issues would be collectively avoided and denied. The skillful therapist is the one who brings important themes and dynamics out into the open, even if it means angering or upsetting members of the group. A therapy group for adult survivors of child sexual abuse is not the place for a professional who is unwilling or unable to take such a risk.

The Therapist Confronts Members' Denial

In the fifth session, Lucy and June were discussing feelings about their mothers. Both women were abused by male family members, Lucy by her uncle and cousin, June by her maternal grandfather. As children, both hinted to their mothers that they were being abused and were ignored. Lucy stated, "I feel like I've moved beyond anger at anyone about the abuse. Really, I think what I need to work on is trusting men and learning how to have normal relationships with them. As far as my mom, I know we will never be close. She just doesn't seem to want it. But that's okay with me now."

"I know what you mean," Lucy responded. "I've been angry and it didn't get me anywhere. I think it really is better to forgive and forget. I'm almost sure that my mother was abused by her father, so how can I blame her for what happened to me? It hardly seems fair."

Two other female members of the group then commented they were envious of Lucy and June, that the two seemed to be making real progress. Members voiced their agreement.

"I know you say that you have dealt with your feelings toward your mothers, but I just have a sense that you haven't even scratched the surface," the therapist responded. "This will probably make you angry and maybe some of the rest of you as well, but I think that both of you still harbor a lot of rage about what happened, about how your mothers could have ignored your cries for help, and how they didn't care enough to see your pain. June, I know that you, particularly, want a relationship with your mother, that you're lonely and want her to be there for you. But wanting it and having it are two different things. I have the feeling that any relationship with her will be on her terms, with you doing all the giving. I believe you're afraid to deal with these feelings."

Fred responded, "There you go again. You're not content unless someone is crying or feeling bad. Isn't it possible they really have dealt with their feelings about their mothers?"

Ben agreed. "Why do you always have to look for problems?" Both Lucy and June admitted their anger with the therapist.

While she said she understood members' anger, the therapist reiterated her observations. "It seems like everyone wants, maybe even needs, to believe that June and Lucy are through with their anger. The problem is, it's just not that simple."

Lucy and June were dealing with overwhelming feelings of rage, sadness, and abandonment in the only way they knew how, by denying them. Others in the group also wanted to believe that working through difficult feelings was as easy as Lucy and June described it. A therapist's ability to be helpful to the group resides in a willingness to confront these issues. It is unrealistic and inappropriate to expect the group to identify and confront such collective denial without the therapist's assistance.

MODELING APPROPRIATE BEHAVIOR

The therapist's role in culture building extends to setting examples through her or his own behavior. The rules to guide the group must be consistent with the therapist's own actions and the expectations he or she holds for the members.

Inconsistency between the group therapist's actions and her or his stated expectations leads to confusion and members are likely to blame themselves. Members tend to rely upon the therapist's nonverbal behavior to determine what is expected of them. The stated goal of a group may be, for example, to work on members' feelings of rage and sadness. However, if the group therapist is uncomfortable with honest expression of these feelings, members inevitably know and refrain from such discussion.

Survivors enter group therapy already burdened with low self-esteem and feelings of inadequacy. They are frightened and overwhelmed by their feelings and only too ready to view themselves as "crazy" and abnormal. Further, survivors are often faced with disbelief and denial when they attempt to disclose their abuse or discuss their feelings about it. The group culture, as embodied in the therapist's own expectations and actions, should neither reinforce these feelings nor invalidate survivors' sense of reality. When there is inconsistency between the group therapist's stated norms and the actual expectations that guide the group, not only is the resulting group experience likely to be counterproductive, it may actually be harmful.

The therapist's behavior must reflect the norms that have been specifically established which promote member growth. As noted, for example, the therapist should urge all members to be as honest as possible about their feelings, their experiences, and their reactions to and feelings about others in the group. The therapist can model this expectation in the introduction at the beginning of a new group by acknowledging her or his nervousness. This revelation is likely to be met with a collective sigh of relief, as members acknowledge their own anxieties and fears about this new experience.

Throughout the group, the therapist continues to model behavior reflecting the therapeutic norms of the group. While the therapist's behavior in the initial stages of the group is particularly critical in the establishment of the group's culture, his or her actions continue to guide members' behavior.

The Therapist Confronts Denise's Anger

Janet revealed she was often abused by her brothers while her mother entertained a series of boyfriends. Janet finished by saying, "I just can't stand women who sleep around with men. It's cheap. They're cheap." Janet was angry and the therapist asked if Janet considered her mother a "whore." Janet agreed, saying that her mother was no better than a prostitute, leaving Janet to fend for herself.

During this exchange, Denise was quiet but agitated. When the therapist commented on this, Denise launched into a defense of Janet's mother. This was unusual for

Denise, since she typically expressed anger and disgust toward members' parents. Denise then turned to the therapist, and said, "You're damn right I'm angry. I'm pissed at your insensitivity. You know I was a prostitute. Yet you sit there in judgment of Janet's mother and look down your nose at people like me. I'm offended. How dare you?"

The therapist explained to Denise that she was trying to voice Janet's view, not her own view, because of Janet's resentment of women, calling them "cheap" and "sneaky." Denise remained angry, and repeated, "I don't care. You offended me and you have no right to sit in judgment of me."

When the therapist noted that Denise's anger may have more to do with her own unresolved guilt feelings about being a prostitute than about the therapist's use of the word "whore," Denise denied this. She was "furious and deeply offended," she said.

The therapist apologized to Denise, stating she did not mean to offend her and was sorry that she hadn't considered how Denise might feel about her use of the word "whore."

Denise calmed down and accepted the apology. The therapist then processed with group members what had just happened: Janet's anger at her mother and women, in general; Denise's angry response; and the therapist's response to Denise. Members reported being nervous and upset by Denise's anger, particularly since it was directed at the therapist. Two members expressed that they shared Denise's observation that the therapist had been insensitive.

Survivors have deep reservations about expressing anger. Anger, however, is a normal, inevitable aspect of relationships. In this case example, members' concerns about anger were heightened because it was directed toward the therapist. The interchange between Denise and the therapist reinforced the already-established norm of honest communication. Since both Denise and the therapist survived Denise's rage, it demonstrated that anger was acceptable. The therapist's responses provided examples for members in responding to the anger of others. When the therapist acknowledged her mistake, she took responsibility for and validated Denise's anger. When survivors witness the therapist say, "I'm not perfect. I made a mistake, and I'm sorry. Thanks for setting me straight," it is both reassuring and enlightening given their chronic feelings of low self-esteem and inadequacy.

The therapist serves as an important role model to clients in many ways. When it comes to facing difficult issues such as anger, sadness, and accepting responsibility for errors, the therapist's actions and reactions serve as particularly important and instructive guides. Research findings drawn from studies of traditional psychotherapy groups support this view.* Particularly noteworthy is the finding that group members' overall behavioral styles mirror that of the therapist.

PROFESSIONAL USE OF SELF

In both individual and group therapy, the client's relationship with the therapist, as distinct from specific clinical interventions, has the potential to be an important therapeutic tool. Such a relationship is most beneficial when both the client and therapist are authentic and honest in their dealings with one another. From observing and interacting with their therapist,

See, for example: Barlow et al. 1982; Dies 1983; Morrison et al. 1978; Stockton et al. 1986.

clients learn important lessons about intimacy and managing difficult emotions and issues. The therapist's honesty and sincerity convey important messages about their worth and value as individuals.

Therapists who are unwilling or unable to share an authentic, genuine part of themselves, or who remain inappropriately distant from their clients, limit the potential to be helpful. If the therapist's humanness is absent, the validation and affirmation will be missing for the client. Finally, and perhaps most important, the client, at some level, will know if the therapist is not being honest. This knowledge is counterproductive and undermines the therapist's credibility, his or her ability to be helpful, and the client's ability to use the offered assistance.

Nowhere is a therapist's authenticity and genuineness more important than in a group for adult survivors of child sexual abuse. These individuals have been lied to for years. In their childhood, their abusers rationalized and justified the abuse, while their parents, teachers, and other significant individuals denied it. In adulthood, friends and loved ones discount and dismiss the long-term effects of the abuse, while family members continue to avoid it. In addition, many survivors have worked with therapists who may have participated in the deception either by ignoring the abuse or minimizing its impact.

Survivors become skillful at lying to themselves and hiding from others. This reflects their attempts to protect themselves from being "discovered." One of the most common ways that survivors cope is to suppress memories, as well as feelings associated with their abuse. Spontaneous, authentic emotions of any sort are frightening, alien, and avoided.

The therapist's humanness conveys acceptance and validation for clients. The therapist's real feelings in response to real situations are instructive, demonstrate that honesty is acceptable, and encourage members to risk doing the same. If the therapist is unwilling to risk being open, it is highly unlikely that members will do so either. The findings of several studies are consistent with this view and point to the positive relationship that exists between therapist self-disclosure and group cohesion and member self-disclosure (Antonuccio et al. 1987).

The Therapist's Honest but Unexpected Display of Emotion

As the session was getting underway, the author commented that Susan was not looking well, that she looked ill or sad. Susan began crying, and revealed that a good friend of hers, one of her only friends, had died suddenly. Susan reported feeling lost, angry, and overwhelmed. Several other members began crying as well. Several commented that they weren't sure why they were crying, but they were feeling sad, too.

Susan's grief for her friend's death triggered her and other members' sadness over their loss of childhood and innocence. Several members admitted it was difficult to feel these emotions.

The therapist, explaining that grieving over losses was hard for everyone, became teary-eyed and explained to the group that she was working with a young woman who was dying of terminal cancer. While the therapist had not intended to discuss this individual client with the group, nor had she intended to cry, it was clear to the group that she, too, was having a hard time dealing with death.

In this instance, the therapist's reactions were completely honest and spontaneous. While she could have tried to deny or suppress these feelings, she would have sent a wrong, but very powerful, message to the members, since they would have sensed her sadness anyway. Instead, the therapist chose to acknowledge her feelings, and convey to the members that their reluctance to grieve was understandable, since it was hard for her, too. The disclosure was unplanned, but the therapist was able to use the opportunity in a disciplined way to benefit the group. Even if the therapist had not been able to use her spontaneous reactions to the group's advantage, a genuine response was better than no reaction or a dishonest one.

The therapist's disciplined use of self is one of the most crucial skills for successful treatment yet possibly one of the most misunderstood. Clients know intuitively whether their therapist is being honest. The therapist can only demand honesty from clients if she or he is willing to be genuine and authentic. When the therapist admits to making a mistake, members realize they do not have to be perfect either.

It is both the process of sharing with clients and the content of such disclosures that are helpful. In a group for survivors, the therapist may share feelings about and reactions to members' revelations and interactions with one another. For example, this might include the therapist's anger at individuals who have hurt and exploited other members, sadness over members' losses, expressions of regard for the group, and would also include the therapist's acknowledging mistakes. Evidence drawn from research on the impact that the therapist's self-revealing behavior has on psychotherapy groups indicates that therapist's comments conveying caring and regard for the group and its members are perceived as helpful by the members (Wright et al. 1978; Dies and Cohen 1976).

Where appropriate, the group therapist may use life experiences and reactions to events to help members develop a more realistic sense of themselves. Survivors have a distorted and unrealistic perception of what it means to be normal, which means for many being problem-free. The therapist's revelations about challenges she or he has faced assists members in developing a more realistic view of themselves and others. Research findings on this aspect of therapist self-disclosure in group, while scant, suggest that comments which indicate to members that the therapist has experienced normal feelings such as anger, anxiety, and sadness, are helpful (Dies 1983; Dies and Cohen 1976).

FOCUSING ON HERE AND NOW

The therapist has the primary responsibility for helping the group to reflect on itself and the way the members work with and relate to each other. Unlike social relationships that exist outside the group, members can receive feedback about their behavior and can be helped to examine their interactions with each other.

Reflecting on here-and-now experiences is not something individuals generally do in their relationships. Since such reflection is often discouraged, the group therapist should assume that this behavior, crucial as it may be for the effectiveness of the group, will be new and frightening to the members. Survivors are particularly reluctant to examine their immediate experiences, owing to their tendency to hide from others and to mask their true feelings.

The therapist has four interrelated tasks in this regard. First, an environment must be created where a focus on the here and now is encouraged, underscoring the group norm of honest discussion. Second, the therapist's expectations for her or himself and the members must include a focus on the immediate present. Third, members must be helped to experience the here and now. Finally, the therapist must help members to reflect on what happened and its meaning. Through modeling and explicit instruction and guidance, the therapist helps members to examine their interactions with one another as these occur.

If the therapist has been skillful in establishing a group culture that promotes work and growth, this function is increasingly taken over by the group itself. A mature, working group is one where members take responsibility for processing and reflecting on the ways in which they work together. Members cannot be expected to do this, however, unless the therapist has assisted and shown them how.

Bob Confronts the Group

In the sixteenth session, Bob disclosed that more memories about his abuse had emerged. He now knew what he had only suspected before. He remembered he had been sexually assaulted by more than one man at a time, and began to discuss the humiliation and sadness concerning this new memory with the group.

The group seemed uncomfortable with Bob's disclosure and his sadness. Other members' concerns then predominated and Bob remained quiet for the remainder of the session.

As the group was winding down, Bob commented, "I'm disappointed in you guys. You weren't there for me on this one. I wanted to really go into my feelings about the sadness and the shame. You seemed to ignore me. I think I understand why, and I'm not angry. I just think we'd have gotten more work done if you hadn't chickened out."

Bob was not angry as much as he was disappointed, and he clearly conveyed this to the group. Bob also commented on the way members had worked together that session. The response of the group to Bob's observations was equally important. They acknowledged he was right and had avoided important issues. With little assistance from the therapist, they were able to process Bob's feelings about being abandoned and why they had been so reluctant to confront his disclosures.

Balancing the Past and the Present

In a group for adult survivors, the therapist must learn to maintain the appropriate balance between focusing on the past and emphasizing the present. Survivors need to talk about and work through their feelings about the abuse, which requires discussing the past, events and people outside the group's boundaries. However, members also need to work on social relationships, and this is best accomplished by processing their interactions with each other in the here and now. The skillful therapist assists members in seeing how outside events and people influence their reactions and feelings about each other. Using the past to illuminate the immediate present is an important aspect of group work with adult survivors.

PROFESSIONAL SUPPORT
AND SUPERVISION

Therapy with adult survivors is extraordinarily difficult and challenging. In each session the group therapist is confronted with a large array of group and individual dynamics that must be processed simultaneously. The amount of information to be analyzed and the intensity of issues can at times be overwhelming and emotionally draining to the therapist.

The more therapeutic the group, the more emotionally challenging it will be for the therapist. A group that is not demanding to the therapist is more than likely not demanding to the members, either. The pain and rage of survivors are real and acute. The therapist inevitably is touched and affected by these intense, sometimes raw emotions.

Kevin's Story Affects the Therapist

Kevin revealed specifics of his abuse, something he had been rather vague about before. Following the death of his parents, his uncle seduced him less than two months after Kevin went to live with him and his aunt. Kevin was 12 at the time. During the next six years, the abuse progressed from sodomy and oral sex to group sex and, finally, sadomasochism. Kevin was forced to endure enemas, pins and needles inserted into his penis, and objects inserted into his rectum. The sexual abuse became increasingly ritualistic and painful. As Kevin revealed this, he became increasingly anxious, panicky, and teary-eyed, an uncharacteristic response for him.

As she listened to Kevin's story, the therapist became teary-eyed and angry, as well. She shared her reactions with Kevin during the session, but the therapist was still preoccupied with these feelings well after the meeting had ended. Later, the therapist talked with a colleague, and before long, both were crying.

The group therapist needs an outlet for the personal reactions generated by the group session. No matter how experienced, the therapist continues to need to use other professionals as sources of advice, validation, and support.

It is important for the therapist to discuss with other therapists her or his reactions to the group, as well as ask for and receive pertinent, expert feedback and advice about clinical interventions. This increases the likelihood that the therapist will be effective in leading the group and minimizes the effects of countertransference.

3
Creating and Structuring the Group

Referrals for a theme-oriented therapy group for survivors may come from several sources. The group therapist may submit an announcement to local newspapers and community newsletters publicizing the formation of a new therapy group. Other therapists may refer a client for possible inclusion in the group, and some survivors may refer themselves. Clients who are self-referred or referred by family members usually are more likely to complete group than those who are referred by other sources.

SELECTION OF MEMBERS

The ability to relate to others is crucial to a survivor's successful participation in a group and all prospective members should be evaluated for their ability to fit into the group and capability of completing the 20-week sessions. Using the same broad exclusion criteria commonly recommended in the group treatment literature, survivors diagnosed with borderline, sociopathic, and psychotic disorders would be poor candidates for group therapy. Survivors who are acutely suicidal, actively abusing alcohol or drugs, or severely depressed or withdrawn also are not appropriate candidates. Survivors who are brain damaged or mentally retarded would be poor risks for group therapy. Individuals who would be likely to have difficulty connecting and relating to others or might assume a deviant role in the group, a role that would be harmful to both themselves as well as the group, are clearly not suitable candidates for group therapy.

The Pregroup Interview

The therapy group is extraordinarily powerful and not all survivors are capable of handling the intense, often overwhelming, feelings that surface as a result of participation in the group. A pregroup interview is an effective means of determining an individual's readiness and appropriateness for group therapy. Practical issues such as fees also can be discussed. Survivors should not be placed in a situation where they might experience failure.

The pregroup interview provides the group therapist with the opportunity to collect information about the survivor's past history, current situation, as well as previous and current therapy experiences. This data is useful for several reasons. First, and perhaps most importantly, the pregroup interview provides the therapist with valuable insights into the kinds of issues the client needs to work on. It also assists the group therapist in anticipating group and individual dynamics that may emerge if the interested client joins the group.

Carol's Pregroup Interview

Carol, a 42-year-old married mother of three, met with the therapist to discuss her possible involvement in the group. She revealed that she had been molested over a 10-year period by her father, with her mother's tacit knowledge. Her father called his abuse a "love affair" and threatened to harm and sexually abuse Carol's younger sister if Carol refused his advances or told anyone.

When asked about previous experiences with therapy, Carol revealed a troubling history. Carol left home at 19 to get married. Six months later, her younger sister tried to kill their father with a shotgun. The sister was placed in an institution. The institution's male psychiatrist requested interviews with all members of the family, trying to determine why the sister had shot their father. In Carol's interview, the psychiatrist told her the shooting was her fault. After seducing him, he explained, Carol had hurt her father by leaving him to marry another man. This psychiatrist also told Carol she should have known that her father would seduce her sister and she should have done something to prevent it.

Carol also revealed, reluctantly and with a great deal of prodding from the therapist, as she got older, she became sexually aroused when her father abused her. Carol was concerned about revealing her sexual arousal because she was afraid (and understandably so) of what others might think. Gathering this kind of information in the pregroup interview is invaluable. It was crucial for Carol's recovery that she disclose her secret to the group. Only then could she receive the validation, reassurance, and acceptance she needed. Armed with this knowledge, the therapist could help Carol work on her guilt in the group.

Carol's story exemplifies the value of the therapist asking about sensitive, painful matters in the pregroup interview. When such questions are posed to survivors, they provide the therapist with valuable background knowledge concerning the client's treatment needs. Questions should be accompanied by an explanation concerning why such information is needed; this not only helps to alleviate clients' fears, it also enhances the likelihood their responses will be honest.

Survivors' willingness and ability to disclose their abuse in the pregroup interview is a good indication of how they will function in a group setting. Survivors who are completely incapable of discussing their abuse are generally poor candidates for the group. If the survivor has difficulty discussing the abuse in a one-on-one situation, it is likely that she or he will experience similar problems sharing the past with others. Inability to discuss the abuse suggests that the client is neither ready nor able to explore her or his victimization, much less the feelings associated with it.

A client's ability to discuss the abuse as a selection criterion might suggest that clients with memory loss about their abuse would be inappropriate candidates. This is not necessarily the case, however. Even though these individuals may lack specific recollections, they nonetheless suffer from a variety of other problems typically associated with survivors. If they are able to talk about the difficulties they are experiencing, they should be considered as possible candidates for group treatment.

Sally's Vague Recollections of Abuse

Sally, 29, referred herself at the suggestion of her mother, also a survivor. At the time of her initial interview, she had only a vague recollection of her abuse. She recalled being raped by her cousin when she was age 12, although the details were unclear. She also had an indistinct memory of french-kissing her uncle when she was eight or nine. As she disclosed these experiences, Sally became increasingly upset and anxious. She began crying, but said, "I'm not even sure why I'm crying." Sally suspected there was more to her abuse than she could remember but also felt it was the right time to face these issues.

Sally has been a member of several groups since this initial interview and continues to profit from them. She now has more complete memories of her victimization at the hands of her grandmother and uncle. Even when these memories were still fragmentary, she was able to relate effectively and freely with others in the group. As she had in her pregroup session, Sally often found herself crying or getting angry in the group, even though she wasn't exactly sure why. Group discussion prompted the gradual return of several painful memories, which was less frightening for Sally because of the support, encouragement, and understanding of the group.

Even when survivors have an incomplete knowledge of their abuse, they often have a basic, largely unconscious, awareness of their victimization. Survivors who believe they have a full, complete memory of their abuse often have repressed certain painful aspects or have other forgotten abusive experiences. It is appropriate for the therapist to inquire whether prospective group members have any unexplained feelings or thoughts about their abuse in the pregroup interview.

One technique is to ask clients whether they have any unexplained pain, particularly in their genital areas. The therapist also may ask survivors whether certain smells, sensations, places, or people evoke strong, unexplained reactions. This information is often helpful in anticipating and interpreting issues that might emerge in group. Given the disconcerting nature of these questions, the therapist needs to clearly explain the meaning and value of the information.

Preparing Prospective Group Members

The pregroup interview also serves the valuable purpose of explaining to clients the nature and demands of the therapy group. Prior to making a commitment, clients need to have a clear idea of what they are getting into. While survivors may have had prior experience with groups, particularly self-help groups, it is critical that survivors understand how therapy groups differ from other kinds of groups they may have attended. The therapist needs to explain the purpose and value of a therapy group.

Following an explanation of both the therapist's and member's roles and responsibilities, two issues must be addressed: Does the survivor understand and agree with the therapist's perspectives? Is she or he capable of adhering to the rules and structure that the therapist has established? As with all clients, survivors have the right to refuse assistance. Such refusal, however, should only come after the service has been thoroughly explained and its meaning and potential benefits clearly understood by the client.

The therapist should use the pregroup interview to determine whether the survivor is capable of making the necessary commitment and adhering to the required group norms. Some clients are simply not able to meet the demands of the group and the therapist should anticipate that survivors not accepted into the group will be hurt and angry. While it is likely they will feel as if they somehow failed, the sense of failure would be far more acute if they were allowed to enter the group but were unable to deal with its demands and requirements.

The pregroup interview prepares prospective members for the group therapy experience. Such preparation comes not only from what the therapist tells survivors about the group, it also comes from the interview itself, from the way the therapist relates to the client, and what the therapist expects of him or her in this session. The expectations the therapist holds for clients in the pregroup session should mirror those held for members in the group. Through their interaction with the group therapist in this session, prospective members learn what they can expect in the group.

The pregroup interview should be used to prepare members for the first group session where they will be asked to share their stories with one another. This is frightening and the therapist needs to acknowledge and validate this fear with clients in their initial individual session. The therapist should explain that it is only when members are honest about themselves and are then met with support and understanding that they can truly feel accepted and connected to others. With each week that goes by without honest self-disclosure, it becomes harder for such discussion to start. Sharing their stories with the therapist in the pregroup interview assists survivors to do this in the group.

Several studies have examined the value of pregroup preparation for members of psychotherapy groups.* Different types of activities have been used, ranging from individual interviews to video presentations, and results generally indicate that this strategy is associated positively with members' knowledge of and readiness for group, attendance at group sessions, and remaining in group for its duration. Evidence exists suggesting that the pregroup interview is associated with increased participation in the group and member self-disclosure.

Considering the Whole Group

Individual members' experiences and interpersonal styles should complement and enhance the group as a whole. The therapist should strive for heterogeneity with respect to issues such as the survivor's victimization, progress in recovery, age, and the ability to present problems. The power of the group is enhanced and intensified by members' varied experiences and lifestyles. Described below are members of a typical survivor's group.

---

*See, for example: Hilkey et al. 1982; Jacobs et al. 1976; Piper and Perrault 1989; Tolman and Bhosley 1989.

A Group Composite

Gary: Age 26. Single. Sodomized by older brother at the age of nine. Family unaware of the abuse until he was 21. His father (deceased) and brother have a history of alcoholism. Current problems include avoidance of intimate relationships, suicidal and homicidal thoughts, low self-esteem, intense feelings of self-loathing and inadequacy, and sexual dysfunction. One prior experience with individual therapy; not in therapy at the present time. He presents himself as withdrawn and extremely awkward in the presence of others. Has great difficulty maintaining eye contact with others.

Carol: Age 40. Three children. Married 19 years, but in the process of separating. Molested by father over a 12-year period. Abuse included intercourse, pornography, oral and anal sex. She was often orgasmic during the abuse. Told mother when she was 13, but abuse continued. Abuse ceased when she ran away and married at 20. Current problems include low self-esteem, overwhelming feelings of guilt and shame, depression, extreme marital discord, sexual dysfunction, and suicidal thoughts. In group and individual therapy irregularly for four years. Carol is articulate, insightful, and relates easily with others.

Kevin: Age 42. Divorced, two children. Parents died when he was 12. Went to live with aunt and uncle. Uncle began molesting him within two months. Abuse continued until he ran away at 18 and became a male prostitute. Kevin never disclosed the abuse to anyone. Abuse became progressively more sadistic and involved several men. Current problems include confusion over sexual orientation, low self-esteem, acute feelings of inadequacy and self-hatred, depression, self-destructive tendencies, sexual dysfunction, problems with intimacy, and attraction to young boys (not acted upon). No experience with therapy prior to group. He appears extremely nervous, but also is aloof, flippant, and detached from others.

Jean: Age 46. Divorced, three children. Raped by father and his friends at age five. Abuse continued into adolescence. Her father (deceased) and mother have a history of alcoholism. Father also physically abusive. Siblings also physically and sexually abused. Disclosed abuse to mother, but it continued. Jean is a recovering alcoholic. Husband was a batterer and a practicing alcoholic. Current problems include low self-esteem and inability to relate to men. In group and individual therapy for five years. Also actively involved with AA, ACOA, and Survivors of Incest Anonymous (SIA). She is verbal, insightful, and has a warm, engaging manner.

Jeff: Age 32. Divorced, four children. Sodomized by alcoholic father from age eight to approximately age 15 (this just recently remembered). Forced by father to watch as father stripped mother and had intercourse with her; after mother's death, father engaged in same behavior with several other women. Father physically abusive as well. Jeff never disclosed the abuse to anyone. Current problems include suicidal thoughts, low self-esteem, sexual dysfunction, strong feelings of inadequacy and self-loathing, fear of intimacy, and intense feelings of rage. Recovering alcoholic. In group and individual therapy for one year. Also involved in AA and ACOA. Presents himself as very nervous, somewhat hostile, and quiet.

Sally: Age 29. Separated, one child; two step-children. Molested by family members (father, brothers, cousins, and uncles) over a period of at least five years. Female siblings and cousins also molested. Memories about much of the abuse remain fragmented. Father and mother are alcoholics. Father also physically abusive. Husband is alcoholic and physically abusive. Sally never disclosed the abuse. Current problems include low self-esteem, depression, and fear of men and intimacy. Recently, stepson (age 16) charged with molesting a cousin. In group and individual therapy for two years. Also involved in ACOA and Alanon. She is very nervous, anxious, and frightened, particularly in the presence of men.

Fred: Age 41. Divorced, two children. Memories very fragmented and non-specific but suggest sexually seductive behavior on mother's part and possible assault at age seven by a neighborhood boy. At age 17, forced to perform oral sex on an older male friend. Father physically abusive and an alcoholic. Fred is a recovering alcoholic. Current problems include low self-esteem, depression, sexual dysfunction, inability to be intimate, and anger. In group and individual therapy six months. Also involved in AA. Fred presents himself as self-absorbed, distant, and angry, particularly at women.

Joan: Age 38. Divorced, two children. Abused by maternal grandfather over eight- to 10-year period. Abuse included pornography, intercourse, and oral and anal sex. Disclosed to mother, who continued to leave her in care of grandfather. Current problems include problems with intimacy, low self-esteem, and sexual dysfunction. In group and individual therapy irregularly for two years. She is quiet, but insightful and articulate.

What might be most readily apparent from these brief descriptions is members' similarities with respect to presenting problems. Despite having been sexually exploited in very different ways, survivors share many common problems, and it is this commonality that forms the core of the group.

All of these clients shared problems with low self-esteem. Most had significant problems with emotional and sexual intimacy. A number of the members also experienced serious problems with depression and were plagued by thoughts of suicide. A few were struggling openly with intense feelings of anger, and several with powerful feelings of self-loathing. Finally, a number of them were in recovery for alcohol or substance abuse.

If their underlying sameness bonds the group, survivors' differences provide the group with its energy — gathering forces for change. For example, several members of this group had disclosed their abuse to their mothers, but the abuse continued. The collective rage at their mothers along with heightened feelings of betrayal and abandonment became the focus of many group discussions. Several other members who had never disclosed their abuse but were nevertheless angry at their mothers or others for letting it happen also were able to acknowledge and work on this.

Jeff, who had spent a great deal of time being angry at his father, was beginning to realize how strong his hatred was toward his mother for not protecting him. Jeff's realization, as well as that of others in the group, was stimulated by his interacting with and hearing individuals whose "stories" were different from his.

Similarly, because of the nature of his abuse and later involvement in prostitution, Kevin's feelings of self-loathing and disgust were particularly acute. As he articulated these feelings as well as the nature of the abuse, other members of the group were able to talk about their own sense of humiliation and shame. This discussion was painful and intense, and it is doubtful that it could have taken place had someone like Kevin not been in the group.

Diverse experiences also help members reduce their feelings of isolation. As members disclose their abuse to each other, it becomes more difficult for them to adhere to the belief that they are alone. They learn quickly there are others like them. Hearing others describe their victimization not only provides members with a sense of universality, it also helps them gain a better, more accurate perspective on their own abuse.

For example, Fred questioned whether he even was a survivor, since the only distinct memory he had involved a friend. He asked "Am I a survivor of sexual abuse if I was 17 and the guy was a friend?" As others in the group described very different experiences, Fred was able to recognize that he was, indeed, a survivor, because, as he said, "This is eerie. You people seem to feel exactly like I do, even though what happened to you was so different."

In a treatment group for men and women, it is important that neither sex feel "outnumbered." Survivors are keenly aware of gender and whether there are more or fewer men or women in group. The therapist should strive to achieve approximately even numbers of men and women and be sensitive to members' concerns when there is an imbalance.

Considering Perpetrators for the Group

One troublesome issue that merits discussion is that of survivors who are perpetrators. In the pregroup interview, the therapist should consider exploring this issue with both men and women. The therapist should, however, be wary about the veracity of the information that is obtained at this time, owing to clients' understandable reluctance to acknowledge and accept responsibility for such behavior.

Kevin Discloses His Risk for Offending

In his pregroup interview, Kevin acknowledged that as an adult he was tempted to offend his nephew; it was this experience that prompted him to seek treatment. He subsequently shared this in the group. His disclosures prompted powerful, honest discussions of sexuality, and, in each case, group members responded with understanding, support, and validation. Several other members, male and female, discussed sexual encounters that they initiated with younger children when they were minors, encounters which caused great shame and guilt.

Accepting an acknowledged perpetrator is problematic and the therapist needs to assess the impact this individual would have on the group and the group would have on him or her. An acknowledged perpetrator would generate a great deal of anger from the group, and while this might be a powerful stimulus for work, it would also target this individual to be the scapegoat and set him or her up to fail.

Another consideration would be the perpetrator's commitment to treatment, acceptance of responsibility for his or her actions, whether the pedophilia was ongoing or in the past, and whether the individual was known to the criminal justice system. Someone already known to the criminal justice system would present fewer challenges than one who is not. Under most circumstances, and with the knowledge of the client, the therapist would be obligated to report a perpetrator's actions to the appropriate legal authorities. A perpetrator whose offending behavior occurred in the past and who demonstrates an ability to control this behavior would be a better candidate for group than one whose sexually abusive behavior was more recent and whose ability to control such behavior is questionable.

Family Members as Group Members

A somewhat less troublesome issue concerns including members of the same family in a group. In the case of siblings, as long as both meet the selection criteria and are comfortable with their joint participation, there is no reason why they can't join. In the case of a parent and child, where both are survivors, the potential impact their presence would have on the group would have to be assessed carefully. It is possible the inevitable conflict and hostility that exist in their relationship would be a diverting influence on the group, even though the potential for this tension to deepen the group's work also exists.

Research on Group Composition

Several studies have explored issues related to group composition.* Research examining the impact of homogeneous versus heterogeneous groups has produced ambiguous results but there is evidence suggesting that clients derive greater benefits from groups in which there is heterogeneity with respect to member personalities and ability levels. Groups where the majority of members could be characterized as expressive and person-oriented seem to be more helpful. At least one study of men and women who participated in a divorce adjustment group found that the therapeutic benefits concerning the curative factor, instillation of hope was enhanced by members being in different stages of their recovery (Bell et al. 1989). There also is evidence to indicate that more homogeneous groups with respect to a variety of interpersonal characteristics of members have higher rates of attendance. Finally, research findings indicate that individuals are more likely to drop out if their

---

*See, for example: Melnick and Woods 1976; Klein and Carroll 1986.

interpersonal, behavioral style deviates from the style that predominates in the group.

Research in group treatment has explored variables associated with member drop out.* Clients whose interpersonal skills are extremely deficient, as well as those who are overly aggressive, withdrawn, or mistrustful are particularly likely to drop out. Clients who demonstrate weak motivation for treatment, have little or no prior experience with therapy, or who have unrealistic expectations regarding group also are poor risks. Individuals drop out at a higher rate if they are faced with situational barriers to attending group, such as work conflicts and day-care problems.

Two recent studies have explored predictors of successful group participation for female survivors (Follette et al. 1991; Neimeyer 1991). In the first study, results indicated several variables were predictive of members' poor response to group: lower educational level, a history of oral-genital abuse or intercourse, poor level of adjustment prior to group treatment, and being married at the time of group treatment. Duration of the abuse and other factors associated with the survivor's family of origin were not predictive of outcome. In the second study, a less positive outcome was associated with members who displayed a pessimistic or negative outlook in group, had a reduced capacity to identify with other members of the group, and perceived other members or the leader in extreme, polarized terms.

One 1991 study explored the relative merits of process-oriented and structured time-limited group formats for female survivors (Alexander et al. 1991). For women who had never been in therapy or had never disclosed the abuse, the more structured format controlled anxiety, increased members'

---

*See, for example: Bostwick 1987; Horenstein and Houston 1976; Klein and Carroll 1986; Roback and Smith 1987.

feelings of comfort, and minimized member conflict. The process group was found to be an appropriate option for women with prior therapy experiences.

GROUP SIZE

The ideal size for a therapy group for survivors is seven to eight members. A group of seven to eight people is small enough to facilitate members' becoming close to one another. It is large enough, however, to somewhat mitigate the disruptive effects that member absences have on the group. Inevitably, members miss group from time to time, due to illness, work responsibilities, and the like. In a group smaller than seven, the absence of even one member is keenly felt by all. Having too many members is likely to be a greater problem than too few. A large group is threatening to members and makes intimacy between them more difficult. It also places more demands on the therapist. The array of individual and group dynamics can become overwhelming in a larger group. The more members in the group, the less time each has to express their views and discuss their problems, and frustration results in individual issues not getting sufficient attention.

A small group provides the ideal environment where feelings of intimacy and connectedness can develop. A group experience has the potential to provide members with the chance to work through long-standing issues associated with their families of origin, an advantage maximized in a smaller group which resembles a family. A smaller group provides each member with sufficient opportunity to concentrate on the issues on which they need to work and places fewer demands on the therapist.

TIME LIMITS

A time-limited, closed therapy group for survivors enhances client commitment, motivation to work, and reduces the risk of drop out. This is important for adult survivors, since they have typically been struggling for years to overcome their childhood experiences, and is consistent with a growing body of literature dealing with group treatment generally.* Time-limited groups have been found to facilitate the rapid development of cohesion, self-disclosure, and feelings of intimacy. Finally, the research available on time-limited groups indicates that, on a variety of outcome measures, clients in time-limited groups do at least as well as those who have participated in open-ended or long-term groups.

The therapy group experience is intense, demanding, and emotionally challenging to its members. Many survivors have had unsuccessful, at times harmful, experiences with therapy; time limits make it easier for members to meet this challenge successfully. The work of the group begins more quickly and lasts much longer when members know that they will be meeting only for a limited time.

Time-limited groups also minimize client dependence and foster self-sufficiency. A common long-term consequence of child sexual abuse is an intense feeling of inadequacy and a therapeutic experience where the end date is known at the outset is reassuring to survivors, who desperately need to feel powerful, efficacious, and in control of their lives.

A closed group provides a much safer environment where members can share painful and sensitive information with each other. All members start together and finish together. This

---

*See, for example: Budman and Demby 1983; Budman et al. 1985; Burlingame and Fuhriman 1990.

experience fosters the sense of "we-ness" so critical to a successful group experience. A closed group avoids the disruptive and negative impact on group process that occurs when a member leaves or a new person joins. Finally, in a closed group, members grow together, and are equally responsible for the way in which the group works. More so than in an open group, a closed group enhances the likelihood that members quickly and strongly come to view the group as theirs.

GROUP DURATION

Decisions regarding group length determination may be somewhat arbitrary. However, a group lasting at least 20 weeks seems to provide maximum benefits to members. Whatever the group's duration, members need to have sufficient opportunity to get close to and feel comfortable with each other. Once this level of comfort and intimacy is established, the most difficult work can take place. Few survivors will have all of their treatment needs met through a single 20-session group experience, and members should have the opportunity to join a subsequent group.

SESSION LENGTH

A group lasting two hours in length is appropriate. This includes formal group time and time at the end to unwind and achieve some sense of closure. A formal period of at least 90 minutes provides members with sufficient time to work on the issues at hand. A shorter group session may leave members feeling they were just starting to talk seriously. Formal sessions that continue much beyond 90 minutes, and certainly beyond two hours, lose their potency quickly as both members and therapist become tired and unfocused.

Given the sensitive nature of the material that surfaces in the group, the therapist should anticipate that "doorknob" comments and behaviors will be common. Further, some of the more important material and group processes are likely to occur later in the session, as members reconnect with one another. Members need time to unwind and "decompress." When the group formally ends, members may need to spend 10 to 15 minutes chatting informally with one another.

The therapist can help the group stay within the time limits by informing members when there are 20 to 30 minutes left in the session. This may mean interrupting a very intense exchange or discussion. However, this time check is helpful to members in beginning the process of winding down.

GROUP GOALS

Given the relatively short-term, time-limited nature of the group, members' goals must be specific and focused in nature. In general, the group should provide all participants with hope for the future and motivation to continue in their recovery. The group also should supply all members with a sense of validation and affirmation, bolstering their sense of worth and self-esteem, and provide an opportunity to feel connected to others.

For most participants, a primary goal will be to work on relationship issues; this goal may be particularly directed at improving relationships and feelings about the opposite sex. For all members, an important goal is likely to be to become more aware, accepting, and less frightened of their feelings regarding the abuse, and to understand how these feelings manifest in their current lives. For many members, the group also will serve as a stimulus for the return of memories. In addition, the group can be helpful to members as they decide upon future courses of therapy.

In the pregroup interview, the therapist should spend time helping prospective members articulate their goals for the group, an often difficult task for clients. Many have not been in group therapy before and have no idea how the group works. Some survivors are overwhelmed and confused by their experience and the resultant feelings, and do not know where to begin. Even those individuals who have previously been in therapy often need the therapist's guidance and assistance to develop realistic goals for themselves.

In a time-limited group, members should have the option of joining a subsequent group. Prior to the start of the new group, these individuals should be encouraged to think about what they expect/need to get out of the next group. For many, the goals may remain the same from one group to the next. For others, there may be a shift in focus, based on changing circumstances in their lives or on issues that emerged in the group.

Examples of Members' Goals

Each member worked on specific goals which were initially identified in the pregroup interview and provided a beginning structure to his or her participation in the group.

Gary: 1.   To acknowledge and explore his feelings
                associated with his abuse.

2. To begin to connect to others and experience some measure of comfort in relationships with others.

3. To reduce his sense of isolation and feelings of being "crazy" and "weird."

Carol: 1. To decide about separating from her husband, and follow through on this decision.

2. To work on her intense feelings of guilt, shame, and responsibility regarding the abuse.

3. To feel more connected to others and less isolated.

4. To begin confronting and exploring her feelings about men.

Jean: 1. To work on her feelings of sadness and pain associated with the abuse.

2. To decide whether or not to confront her mother about the abuse and her mother's inaction at the time it occurred.

3. To begin to explore her feelings about sex and her sexuality.

Jeff: 1. To vent feelings and feel less frightened of anger associated with the abuse.

2. To explore feelings of shame associated with the abuse.

3.   To develop a more complete memory of
      the abuse.

4.   To reduce feelings of isolation and feel
      more connected to others.

Joan: 1.   To explore feelings about her sexuality.

2.   To acknowledge and become less frightened
      of her feelings associated with the abuse,
      particularly sadness and anger.

3.   To explore her feelings about men.

All at various stages in their recovery, each group
members' needs are reflected in their individual goals. For
individuals such as Gary, the goals reveal his inexperience with
therapy and the fact that he was only just beginning to
acknowledge what happened to him. Two-and-one-half years
later, Gary's goals became more refined and focused.

Gary: 1.   To vent his feelings of anger at his family
      for the abuse and at his mother, particularly,
      for not protecting him.

2.   To confront his feelings of inadequacy with
      women.

3.   To begin to acknowledge his sadness
      regarding his abuse.

4.   To develop a more complete memory of
      his abuse since Gary now senses he was
      sexually abused more frequently than he
      had originally recalled, and that his father
      may have abused him as well.

On the other hand, it is clear from Jean's and Carol's goals that they were already working on feelings about their abuse. These women had confronted and were beginning to come to terms with some of the more intense feelings associated with the abuse; each entered with a clear idea about the feelings on which they needed to work. However, they also had identified additional issues they felt they needed to begin to address.

Goals provide both members and therapist with a sense of direction as the group gets underway. However, the therapist, as well as the members, must remain flexible in their adherence to these objectives. As members reveal more about themselves, new issues often emerge — issues which then become the focus of the survivor's efforts.

When Joan started in the group, she had not confronted her feelings about the abuse. She acknowledged she used a number of defenses to keep herself from feeling much of anything. As the group progressed, it became obvious that a particularly difficult issue for Joan was her reluctance to view her mother as responsible for the abuse. An evolving goal for Joan became confronting her mother's complicity in the abuse and deciding whether or not she wanted to confront her mother about this.

When Carol started this group she needed to work on guilt feelings. As the group progressed, this goal was refined as Carol discovered a particularly damaging aspect of her guilt was her shame regarding her sexuality. Carol was embarrassed by her femaleness, ashamed of her sexual feelings, and labeled herself a "slut," which became an important focus of Carol's work.

Some treatment issues only become apparent as members interact with one another. For example, prior to starting the group, Jean identified several goals revolving around feelings about the abuse and herself. This was the first time Jean had been in a therapy group with men, and her anger, fear, and distrust toward men surfaced almost immediately. It became apparent to Jean that much of her work would be directed at her feelings of rage toward men and this quickly took precedence over the goals Jean had initially identified for herself.

Similarly, Jeff entered the group intent on confronting his rage about the abuse. However, Jeff experienced strong reactions to both the men and women in the group, reactions that were getting in the way of his effectively connecting with others. He was often angry at the men, frequently taunting and trying to provoke irate responses from them. On the other hand, he seemed frightened of the women in the group. Upon exploring this, it became clear that much of his anger at his father was directed at men, generally, and the male members of the group, particularly. Jeff's discomfort toward the women in the group stemmed from his fears that, like his father, he might hurt them, he "wasn't really a man," and all women would betray him as his mother had. Jeff also had to begin to work on his tendency to sabotage his relationships with both men and women.

GROUP NORMS

There are several guidelines that are critical to a successful group experience. These are consistent with other types of therapy groups as well as those described in the literature dealing with survivor groups.

Honesty

Members must be encouraged to be as honest as they possibly can with themselves and with each other. Without honesty, no real work can take place. It is only when survivors are able to be truthful with one another that a real sense of connectedness can develop. The mutual-aid function of the group is enhanced when members are honest and confront each other. As members candidly discuss their abuse, feelings associated with it, and the secrets they are working on, they can begin to feel accepted and validated.

Commitment

Members should be required to commit themselves to the full 20 weeks. Clients who have reservations about joining, either because of scheduling conflicts or because they are simply reluctant to make such a commitment, should be dissuaded from participating.

Once a commitment is made, members need to attend all meetings, and inform the therapist if, for any reason, they aren't able to attend. Due to illness and other unexpected events, absences will occur. It is important for members to inform the therapist if they cannot attend, and this information should be relayed to the group. Otherwise, the therapist and the members who are present may be distracted by concerns about the missing member, wondering if there is a problem.

Members quickly come to care about each other and member absences are sources of worry. When someone misses the group, those present often feel both abandoned and resentful.

Addressing a female member of the group who had inexplicably missed the last session, Bob's comments are illustrative: "I'm so glad to see you. I thought something must have happened. But then I also thought, 'What? Aren't we good enough for her? Who does she think she is, anyway?' " In this instance, the absent member had been ill; even so, others in the group experienced feelings of both concern and anger.

The members who are present are not the only ones who are affected by an individual's absence. That individual is influenced as well. The group moves quickly, and missing even one week may leave the absent member feeling lost or disoriented when they return.

Initially, many survivors do not seem to fully appreciate the importance of attendance. Perhaps related to feelings about themselves, members find it hard to believe that others miss them or that it makes a difference when they are absent.

When Members Consider Quitting

When members contemplate quitting, they must discuss this in the group. The group is difficult work. Even with the therapist's screening and prior preparation, the reality of the group may prove too demanding and threatening for some. For others, the issues raised in a particular session may cause them to consider quitting.

Members should discuss any concerns about leaving with the group for several reasons. The feedback and assistance the survivor receives from the group may assist him or her in clarifying what's wrong. Members often consider quitting when the group's work focuses on a particularly relevant issue. Advice, support, and insights of members can be invaluable not only in helping the survivor to understand the reluctance to continue, but also in assisting him or her in persevering. While the aim of such discussion is not to get people to change their minds, it often serves this purpose. No one should be forced to continue, if she or he really can't handle the group experience. On the other hand, for most survivors the issue has less to do with the inability to continue than with the fear about continuing. Fears are best addressed in the group directly, where other members can both acknowledge their own concerns about the process and encourage the individual to finish. In most cases, this is precisely what happens.

Denise Decides to Quit

Denise hid behind a tough exterior, she presented herself as callous, but inside she was as scared and frightened as a little girl. For several sessions, different members of the group had been confronting Denise, suggesting that she was not being honest with herself or with them about her feelings.

"I want to see the real Denise," Bob said. "The 'hard' Denise reminds me so much of my mother, I could strangle you sometimes."

Janet noted, "You always seem like you don't care, so cold-hearted."

Denise became very angry, accusing the group of jumping on her and "singling her out." She said she felt like quitting. While the group processed this with her, Denise was still thinking of leaving even as the session ended.

The following week Denise was able to acknowledge her anger at the group and her fears about where the group was taking her. "My entire life I have had to be strong, to protect myself and my sisters," she told the group. "I've trained myself not to care, not to feel. Otherwise, I think I could go crazy. It's my protective shield. It's hard to give it up, even a little bit."

Denise did not quit the group. The understanding and support she received both about her behavior and about her desire to quit were crucial to her decision. She was frightened when the group asked her to drop her defenses. Yet, such a request was not only justified, it was an important aspect of Denise's recovery. Denise presented herself as an angry, unfeeling woman, detached and aloof from others. She was, however, very lonely and depressed.

For some members, the desire to quit may be justified. When this is the case, it is the therapist's responsibility to help them do so in a way that minimizes their sense of failure and guilt. The member should be encouraged to attend one final session to say goodbye. A number of feelings may be avoided or at least minimized when the survivor has the opportunity to end with the group. Continuing members can be helped to see that the individual's departure is not their fault. Helping the survivor to say goodbye and articulate his or her reasons, as well as validating these reasons, alleviates the sense of guilt and failure.

This is not easy, but it is preferable to the alternative, which leaves all parties concerned with difficult feelings. The remaining members alternate between wondering what they have done to drive the individual away, and being angry at being abandoned. The individual who leaves feeling guilty about quitting, worries about what the others think, sure that she or he has failed again.

Requiring members to speak with the group if they are contemplating quitting protects the interests of both the individual and the group. In most cases, discussion leads to the individual's decision to remain. In those cases where she or he does leave, this requirement provides all members with a chance to work through their feelings, and reduce the sense of guilt, anger, responsibility, and failure that may result.

Confidentiality

Members must adhere to the norm of confidentiality. Issues discussed in the group must stay in the group. Since members' disclosures are sensitive and painful, these can only be made when members are sure that what they have to say is confidential. It is unlikely that the confidentiality requirement will be violated, since this is a strong source of comfort and reassurance to members.

The confidentiality requirement applies to the therapist as well. While the therapist needs to consult other colleagues about the group, it would be ill-advised for the group therapist to discuss members with their individual therapists, unless there is a compelling reason to do so (for example, suicidal ideation) and the member is aware of this.

Limiting Outside Contact

Survivors should be encouraged to avoid or limit their outside contacts with each other. Members' relationships outside of the group can lead to sub-grouping and in-group/out-group issues that have a divisive impact on the group as a whole. Such contact can foster strong, personal feelings between members, feelings that may make it difficult to speak honestly and openly in the group.

If members reside or work in the same community some contact may be inevitable. In this case, the requirement would be for members to limit contacts with one another and avoid discussing group issues. Given the difficulties members have in confronting one another and expressing their anger in group, the risk that such issues would be discussed outside of group is high. Members need to understand that outside discussion of group issues dilutes the power and helpfulness of the group.

Revealing Issues to the Therapist Outside of Group

Members should understand if they bring an issue up with the therapist outside of group, they will ultimately have to bring it up in the group. Private disclosures should be discouraged because they encourage the member to turn to the therapist and not the group. They will occur however, and when they do, the therapist should listen, then remind the individual that he or she needs to share the information with the group.

Such disclosures typically concern extremely painful or embarrassing issues. Speaking to the therapist suggests, at some level, the member wants to share the information with the group. In most instances, the member's behavior should be interpreted to mean that he or she needs the help of the therapist to share the information with the group. While the therapist should not make the disclosure for the client, it is the therapist's role to help the survivor get to the point where he or she can disclose the issue to the group.

The kind of information members are likely to reveal to the therapist outside of group concern feelings that one member has about another, feelings that a survivor has about the therapist, or a painful, embarrassing issue the member is reluctant to discuss. Helping members discuss personal concerns in the group proves to be beneficial to the individual as well as the group. An important benefit of a therapy group for survivors lies in the group process and the opportunities members have to work on their relationships with one another and the therapist. This benefit is compromised to the extent that member concerns are addressed outside of the group sessions.

John Angers Peter

At the end of a session, Peter asked if he could talk with the therapist for a few minutes. He revealed that he was angry with another member, John. Peter knew he should have brought it up in the group, but just couldn't. Peter said he wasn't sure why he was angry, that he felt crazy, and he was afraid to get angry. It didn't seem fair to dump this on John, he said. The therapist suggested Peter's concern for John provided him with an excuse not to explore his anger, and suggested that it would be helpful to both Peter and John to explore this in the group. Peter responded, "I knew you would say that. But you're right." In the next session, with help, Peter was able to tell John how he was feeling.

John reminded Peter of himself, and he didn't like what he saw. Being able to talk and work through this in the group was clearly helpful to him. It also was instructive to the group, since all members experienced problems with anger, often directing it at innocent parties. Peter's disclosure led to an honest and intense discussion of members' feelings about themselves.

Adam Discloses His Secret

Between group meetings, the therapist received a telephone call from Adam, a young member of the group who had been fairly silent in the first six weeks of meetings. He had introduced himself, and disclosed that he had been assaulted by a priest when he was 10, but had revealed little else about himself. He felt strange about the group, he told the therapist, and was not sure he fit in. When asked why, Adam said he thought he must be the only one who was gay, since no one else had yet discussed this. He also felt sure that he was the only one who had been sexually aroused during the abuse, about which Adam felt great shame.

The therapist assured Adam he was not alone on either of these issues. These things were very hard to talk about, she said, and encouraged him to bring these up in the next session, noting that she was sure members would respond with acceptance and relief, the therapist assured him, since she knew others had similar concerns. With help, Adam was able to bring this up at the next session.

Adam's disclosures were sensitive and embarrassing, thus explaining his reluctance to reveal them to the group. He wanted to share these "secrets" with members, but was afraid of their reactions. In a sense, his disclosures to the therapist could be viewed as a test for sharing the information with the group. Not only could he see for himself how another might react, he could also enlist the help of the therapist in sharing this with the group.

It was essential that Adam share his past and present life with the group. He needed their support, acceptance, and validation. Getting these reactions from the therapist was not enough, nor would this have been consistent with the purpose of the group. While the therapist had to provide a great deal of help to Adam in the session that followed his phone call, the response he received from the others was overwhelmingly positive. What followed was a frank discussion of members' sex lives and confusion about sexual orientation. Several members revealed they been sexually aroused during the abuse and several others revealed they had been involved in homosexual relationships, as well.

June Confronts the Therapist

The day before the group was to meet, the therapist received a call from June, who reported that she was not sure she would return to the group. June explained that in the last session she felt the therapist acted like a "know-it-all," insisting June must still be angry with her mother for not stopping her abuse. June continued, "How do you know so much? Maybe I really have forgiven my mother. Anyway, right now, I need her. I have no one else, so I can't deal with being angry with her." Acknowledging June's anger, the therapist suggested June bring this up in the group, since others also became angry for similar reasons. June agreed and with little help, was able to express her anger at the next session.

June's anger toward the therapist reflected her fear about acknowledging anger toward her mother. The therapist had repeatedly pressed her on this issue since June's mother continued to use her and undermine her at every turn. While June was understandably afraid to confront the therapist it was important for her to do this with the other members of the group present. It was important for the group to witness a member confronting the therapist, and both surviving.

Members' Involvement in Individual Therapy

While the therapist may not routinely require group members to be in concurrent individual treatment, she or he may wish to urge clients to consider this option. In the pregroup interview, the therapist should review the client's previous and current experiences in therapy and, for those not involved in individual therapy, caution that the group's work may raise issues that can not be fully explored in a group format.

If the therapist observes a member who seems to be struggling during the group, she or he should once again discuss this issue in and outside the group, if necessary. Pressure from group members may be quite helpful in persuading a member to seek individual treatment. The therapist, of course, should assist with the referral.

PHYSICAL SPACE FOR THE GROUP

Where the group takes place is a significant consideration for survivors groups given their intense nature, the kinds of issues discussed, and the privacy required. Members need to feel their disclosures and discussions cannot be overheard. The requirement regarding confidentiality must be supported by a physical environment members believe is secure.

The environment also must be conducive to and promote honest displays of emotion. Members often need to release painful and angry feelings. Outlets for these displays should be available for members to pound their fists on floors, doors, sofas, or cushions. Tissues should be handy and highly visible. Members need to be encouraged to vent their emotions in ways that do not hurt themselves, others, or the furnishings.

4

The Beginning Phase

The therapist's actions and interventions are critical in the early sessions as the stage is set for the later efforts of the group. The leader's energies should be focused on fostering a sense of commonality among members by encouraging honest discussion and confronting members' anxieties and concerns directly. The therapist should be sensitive to members' expectations for the group, help them to be realistic, and prepare them for possible feelings of disillusionment as the reality of the group sets in. Finally, the therapist must pave the way for the group's focus on itself, since this is critical to an effective group experience.

The therapist's warmth, genuineness, and skill are crucial to the overall success of the group. The therapist serves as a model, establishing and maintaining expectations for members in the beginning sessions when members must rely on the therapist for guidance, observing how they are to work together.

A number of themes in groups for survivors reflect the unique nature of these groups and the members who participate in them. For example, a conspicuous aspect of the early sessions is the hostility and suspicion that surrounds members' feelings toward individuals of the opposite sex. Survivors are not the only clients to hold such misgivings. However, this distrust is so common and often so acute among survivors that it is an important theme and one that drives members' earliest contacts with each other.

While the dynamics and issues in the beginning weeks are apparent in both mixed groups and those containing only women, groups with men and women are much more intense and painful for members. Mixed-sex groups are able to engage in more explicit issues such as rage, loss, and sexuality. Because the presence of both men and women creates so much more tension and energy, certain dynamics are likely to be more pronounced in the mixed groups.

THE USE OF AN AGENDA

Setting an agenda in advance, no matter how flexible, inhibits the spontaneous, natural responses of group members. Deep, genuine feelings do not emerge simply by command, they are triggered by members' ongoing interactions and reactions to each other. However, many groups for survivors operate with fully developed agendas, flexibly adhered to by the leaders, with topics, such as anger and shame, used in each session to guide the group. Different themes or topics introduced into each group session have merit in groups with an educational focus or for survivors who are not yet ready or willing to handle a more unstructured format.

If the fifth week has been designated as the session to discuss anger, members may be able to talk about anger, but not necessarily feel it. This may provide members with reassurance that their anger is normal, but it does not necessarily help them to vent, manage, or work through it. The expression of rage, one of the more dominant themes in a therapy group for survivors, arises not when the therapist says it will, but when members feel it.

The therapist is instrumental in helping members acknowledge and express rage by identifying their feelings and assisting members in articulating them. Without the therapist's guidance and encouragement, it is doubtful that they would have the strength or courage to risk venting such powerful feelings. The therapist's job is to help members and the group as a whole to fulfill an agenda they have set, not to impose one on them. With the therapist's help, a therapy group for survivors will focus on anger, shame, guilt, loss, and the whole host of feelings that trouble members and will do so far more effectively if these emotions emerge naturally through the course of members' interactions with each other.

Many clinicians report that they run issues-oriented, structured survivors' groups. Their adherence to an agenda may reflect a concern about would happen to the group (and to them) if they did not rely on such a format. This fear is understandable. Groups for survivors are extraordinarily demanding and exhausting for both therapist and members. When spontaneous and real emotions are allowed to emerge naturally — without the artificial constraints imposed by an agenda — powerful issues, raw reactions, and honest interactions emerge far more intensely and frequently. Thus, an agenda for each session is not used in the group treatment approach described in this book.

SESSIONAL REVIEW

The therapist's general opening strategy is to start each week's session by reviewing what happened in the previous one, sharing a sense of group direction, and asking for members' reactions to and feelings about these issues. This involves both process and content comments. The first five minutes or so of the session, the therapist discusses significant revelations and disclosures that have emerged in previous weeks, particularly in the last session, identifies important interactions between members, and assists members in understanding their meaning and significance.

The sessional review serves several purposes. It provides therapists with an opportunity to check out their observations with members. Are members seeing things in the same way? Have they picked up on important themes? Have they missed something? The more mature the group, the more feedback they can be expected to give, and the more instructive the information is.

The feedback adds to the therapist's ongoing assessment of group process. It is not possible for any therapist to pick up on every important theme and dynamic in every session. Asking for members' reactions to the therapist's own assessments of the previous session, specifically, and the group's progress, generally, provides the therapist with some reassurance that, if he or she missed something important, the members will let him or her know.

Jean Responds to the Therapist's Review

As usual, the therapist began the tenth session sharing her observations about the previous one which had focused on members' feelings of guilt and responsibility for their abuse. Several individuals had talked about current relationships with their parents, where they continued to be denigrated and made to feel inferior and defective. The therapist pointed out these issues as well as the underlying sadness she had sensed. She added her suspicion that members still clung to certain illusions about their families, illusions that would have to be shattered if members were going to stop tolerating abuse by their families. As long as members held themselves responsible for their abuse, the therapist concluded, they would continue to put up with their families' slights.

Members listened with interest to her comments, nodding occasionally in agreement. When finished, the therapist asked for comments and reactions. Several members turned to Jean, who had emerged as a strong, internal leader of the group. "Well, I think all that makes sense," Jean said. "But I have to tell you that I'm pissed at you. Last week when Sally was talking about her mother and how she knows she'll get nothing but crap from her even now, you told her, 'You shouldn't feel guilty. You didn't do anything wrong.' You can't tell us how to feel. That's how Sally felt. That's how I feel, even if we shouldn't."

Crediting Jean for confronting her, the therapist apologized, "You'll have to forgive me, sometimes things just don't come out the way I want them to." The therapist also acknowledged that simply being told that they're not responsible for their abuse does not erase survivors' deep, long-standing belief that somehow they caused their victimization. By asking for and being receptive to members' feedback, the therapist became aware of this issue relatively early and was able to deal with it directly.

Another advantage of starting each session with a review is that it places some of the responsibility for the running of the group on the members. While the therapist has the primary responsibility for the group's structure and norms, the members, too, must be encouraged to feel a sense of ownership for the group. Enhancing a sense of mutuality and further augmenting members' commitment to the work of the group, soliciting members' opinions reinforces their responsibility for and stake in their group.

One final advantage of beginning the session with a review is the structure and direction it provides to the group work. As the therapist assesses the group's progress and emerging issues, and articulates these for the participants, he or she is identifying the agenda the group has established for itself, even if the members are not fully aware of it. The therapist's task is to identify and interpret the group's work, which, in turn, provides a focus for their continued efforts. This approach relies on an agenda that grows out of the group's work, and not the therapist's a priori assumptions about which issues the group should address.

Members often have some intuitive sense of where the group is and what the important dynamics are. As active participants in the process, however, it is often difficult for them to articulate these issues without the therapist's assistance. While the more mature and experienced group can be expected to identify certain issues, the therapist remains the individual in the best position, through his or her expertise and relative detachment from the painful work of the group, to pinpoint the most disturbing and sensitive aspects of the abuse and members' responses to it. The therapist must be willing to point out an important theme, even if the group is not yet ready to tackle it. The therapist's role is not just to articulate the agenda the group has established for itself, he or she also bears the responsibility for assisting members in moving forward with it.

RAPID DEVELOPMENT OF COHESION

One of the most notable features of time-limited therapy groups for survivors is the rapid development of cohesion. As with any group, time limits foster rapid group development. Since members know they only have a finite time to work together on their problems, they are highly motivated to get to work.

In the first session, members begin by introducing themselves. They enter the first session convinced they are "the only one," "different," "defective," and "weird." They soon discover they are not alone, as they listen to others tell their stories. The opening group activity sets the therapeutic factor of universality into motion almost immediately. As members come to see their underlying commonality, their sense of mutuality and cohesiveness develops rapidly.

That the group is made up exclusively of survivors also contributes to the rapid development of cohesion. Members' similarities and their shared pain, anger, and distress provide a powerful impetus for an early and strong sense of "we-ness." Joan commented during a first session, "For so long I have felt like I just existed, just floated through life. No one knew me. No one could get close to me. I kept everyone away and everything locked in, like a mannequin. I've been here an hour and already I feel something, like I've found people who I might be able to relate to. It feels so weird, so different, but kind of nice." Joan's comments were prompted by the disclosures of another member, and reveal how important it is for survivors to be confronted with their underlying commonality.

Anxiety and tension predominate in the early sessions, as members fear confronting their pasts and of being with others, particularly individuals of the opposite sex. This initial nervousness may be unpleasant to the participants, however, it fuels many of their earliest interactions and often leads to early, sensitive disclosures, which, in turn, fosters a sense of connectedness among members.

Mary Introduces Herself to the Group

Mary, a returning member, had been in individual therapy since the termination of the last group, and as a result, remembered more of what happened to her as a child. When Mary began therapy, she had almost no memory of her childhood or her abuse. Her memory recurred slowly and steadily. Mary knew several returning members, but there were also several new members.

When it came time for Mary to introduce herself, she nervously began to say her name, age, and marital status. She reported her earliest, although still fragmentary, memory was of her cousin raping her at age 12, while several of his friends watched. She then said that she had remembered being abused by her uncles. Mary ended, saying, "That's it, I guess."

Following a brief pause, Mary said, "No, wait a minute. I might as well tell the whole story. I mean, I think I'd rather just get this over with now instead of having it hang over my head." She then proceeded to reveal in detail the history of her ritualistic and frightening abuse, starting at approximately age three, which included oral, anal, and vaginal intercourse.

Mary was extraordinarily anxious about starting this group. Her participation in the last group had been much easier because, at the time, she had so few memories of the abuse. Now that she had remembered much more, she felt like a "freak," and was acutely afraid of what others would think of her, since her abuse seemed to her to be so "weird" and "crazy." Mary's anxiety prompted her to risk telling everything she remembered. The group responded with understanding and support which helped to alleviate Mary's fears. While some members were frightened by her honesty, Mary's revelations served the valuable function of getting the group started in their work.

TENTATIVE REACHING OUT AND DAWNING COMMONALITY AWARENESS

Members' growing recognition of their commonality emerges during the first several sessions of survivors' groups. Survivors enter the group convinced they are defective, freakish, and completely alone in their misery. This belief changes rapidly as survivors come face-to-face with others like them. In many respects, members' reactions to each other may be best characterized as resembling an "aha" experience. Often quite suddenly and dramatically survivors find they are not alone, there are others who feel like them, think like them, have similar problems — others who, basically, share the same distress.

Many survivors have spent most of their lives convinced they are different. In one 90-minute session, this belief is challenged directly. The more honest the disclosures, the more this conviction is tested. While these early disclosures, no matter how honest and frank, cannot dispel completely survivors' beliefs about themselves, they can effectively introduce some doubts about members' long-held beliefs about themselves.

Members' disclosures foster a sense of commonality, lessen the feeling of being alone, and facilitate reaching out to each other. Social isolation is a common problem for adult survivors. Distance from others protects them from further exploitation and keeps others from seeing their secret side. This need to hide is strong, but like all individuals, survivors also need to feel connected to others. As survivors share their stories, the sense of commonality that begins to develop encourages members to reach out and to begin to look to each other for support and acceptance.

Survivors' desire to reach out to others is acute. Their beliefs about themselves and others may have prevented them from doing this in the past, but they enter group with an intense need to feel connected to others. The group provides members with an outlet for a long-unmet, but intensely felt, need.

A Powerful Group Beginning

One recent group, which began only eight weeks following the last group, had all six previous members returning. Three new members were also set to join, but the day before the group was to start, one of the new members died in an auto accident and another moved to a different state. The group started with six returning members, and one new member. The new member, Gail, had been in previous groups with the therapist and knew one other member of the group.

This group was also unusual because, Peter, one of the members of the group, was a close friend of Mark, the young man who had died in the car accident. Peter was quite upset about the death of his friend and the therapist began this group by discussing the unexpected circumstances of Mark's death and the departure of the other prospective member.

Even though six members knew each other, the nervousness and anxiety so common at the beginning of a new group was present. The one new member changed the composition, and returning members were ambivalent about restarting the difficult work of group. The tone for this session was set early on by the therapist's opening comments. In addition to the standard opening discussion of feelings about starting, rules, and members' anxieties, the therapist shared her sadness about Mark's death. There was a noticeable tension from this discussion of grief and death, and, initially, members did not say anything.

Members began introducing themselves, and their comments were brief but candid. Peter provided a short introduction of himself, but then said, "I just have to talk about this. Mark was like the only friend I have, more like family, really. I've had so few people who I have been able to look to in my life . . . three, actually. The other two are gone, and now so is Mark." Peter became teary-eyed, then began crying. Denise, who was sitting next to him, asked Peter if he wanted her to hold him. He said, "Yes." Denise then hugged Peter while he cried.

Others also became teary-eyed, and the mood in the group was somber. Denise began to cry, and for the first time, discussed in detail the suicide of her then-boyfriend when she was an adolescent. She revealed that she had never talked about it, afraid of what others would think and what she might feel. The boy killed himself while talking with her on the phone. He told her he couldn't go on because she had broken off their relationship due to extreme pressure from her family.

When it was Gail's turn to introduce herself, she, too, provided a short history of herself and her abuse, getting more teary-eyed as she talked. She then began crying hard, and revealed to the group that seven months ago her oldest child killed himself after they had argued.

In this case, the therapist used this unusual beginning of a group to work on sadness and grief. Peter, Denise, and Gail had great difficulty acknowledging their feelings of sadness. In the following session, Peter acknowledged, "I need some help with what I'm feeling. I feel angry, crazy, sad, all together. I think this is what people call grief, but I don't know, I've never felt it before. In the past, when I was supposed to feel something, I just numbed out."

Peter, Gail, and Denise, as well as the others in the group were desperately lonely, isolated, and distressed over their losses. While they may have entered the group frightened of others, they were also quite ready, with little prodding, to reach out, ask for help, and acknowledge their sorrow and pain. The group's actions and reactions served not only to help these three individuals, it moved the group forward and sent three powerful messages. It is acceptable to explore sad, powerful feelings. It is safe to reach out to others. And members will survive the experience.

HEIGHTENED TENSION AND ANXIETY

Survivors often have had many experiences with rejection, exploitation, and disappointment. While hoping their relationships in the group will be different, they are ready to expect the worst. Survivors experience a great deal of anxiety about revealing themselves to others and are particularly threatened by the prospect of working with members of the opposite sex.

In the first several sessions, signs of intense anxiety are particularly apparent. Nervous laughter and idle chatter are quite common. In the pregroup interview, the therapist should prepare clients for these reactions. Anxiety about starting the group is normal, expected, and understandable. In the first session, the therapist might share with members her or his own anxieties about starting with a new group. While this may provide members with some degree of reassurance, the truth is that the group remains frightening and threatening. Members will be required to do things that they have often spent a lifetime avoiding — including confronting their past, acknowledging and venting their feelings, and revealing themselves to others. While the therapist provides reassurance that their fears are understandable, he or she must also allow survivors to have such feelings. Empty promises, such as telling members that group work isn't too difficult, do little to assist survivors in engaging successfully in the group and invalidate their sense of reality.

What will help is the therapist's validating the existence of and justification for their fears, and helping them to talk openly and honestly with each other as quickly as possible. The longer members go without disclosing much about themselves or their abuse, the less likely it is that they will be able to work. Until survivors have revealed something of themselves to others in the group, they will continue to worry about how they will be received. No matter what has been disclosed, or how reassuring the revelations of others are, at some level, the individual continues to believe that, while members may be supportive and accepting of others, when hearing her or his own personal story, they might react differently. This worry and belief gets in the way of connecting with and working in the group.

If this last point seems to contradict members' growing awareness of their commonality and their attempts to reach out to each other, it does not. The disclosures of others are comforting and do contribute directly to members' growing sense of mutuality and willingness to connect to others. Equally important, however, are members' own revelations about themselves and the positive responses they receive from others which provide direct and much-needed reassurance that they are okay. Both experiences help alleviate members' initial anxieties about starting the group.

SUSPICION AND HOSTILITY REGARDING THE OPPOSITE SEX

Survivors also often begin the group with a great deal of anger toward members of the opposite sex. For many survivors, these feelings are not conscious. For example, Jennifer had only been vaguely aware of her rage toward men prior to group. She freely acknowledged her mistrust of them, often referring to men as "lizards and snakes." Once she was in the actual presence of men, Jennifer's long-suppressed anger surfaced quickly, and an unexpected angry outburst at the men in the group surprised her.

For others in the group, suspicion and distrust of the opposite sex may be keenly felt. Both Denise and Janet freely admitted that they "hated" men, warning the men in the beginning they "had better watch out." In this same group, Ben acknowledged that, even though he had been married for 14 years, women "gave him the creeps." He didn't trust women, "they are all liars and manipulators."

While not all survivors exhibit either overt or covert signs of mistrust and suspicion, these feelings are important dynamics in the early sessions. Members make frequent disparaging comments about individuals of the opposite sex, often being careful to exclude the "present company." Although these feelings are rarely acknowledged, the comments often are offensive to members. Members' perspectives regarding gender tend to be very rigid, narrow, and stereotyped, and comments such as "all women are . . ." or "no man is . . ." are common.

In this early stage, it is critical for the therapist to point out members' reactions, their meaning, and the feelings that underlie them. Often, feelings are denied, but members need to know that when they are ready, it is acceptable to talk about their suspicions toward the opposite sex.

As they listen to each other talk, suspicions dissipate quickly. It is hard for women to "hate all men" when they witness the men's pain and anguish. Similarly, it is difficult for men to "suspect all women" as they observe how similar the women in the group are to them. While suspicion and hostility manifest in the earliest phase of the group, these feelings often diminish as members begin to recognize their commonality.

THE "HONEYMOON" PERIOD

While members are anxious and often hostile as they begin the group, they frequently bring with them a sense of expectant optimism about the group's impact on their lives. This may seem to be a positive feature of the beginning group, but it also brings an inevitable let down as the group progresses, and members discover that the group is not the instant healing they had hoped for.

While many survivors have been in therapy for years, this experience is not always productive. Even those survivors who have not had negative experiences with therapy have struggled for years, with or without professional help, to come to terms with their victimization and manage their problems. The prospect of being in a group with others who have suffered in a similar way is appealing.

Group Member Preparation

In the pregroup interview the therapist must be careful to accurately and realistically portray the value of the group and what the survivor may hope to get out of it. The therapist must help clients establish feasible and attainable goals given the time frame of the group and the potential for group therapy to effect change.

Clients often enter the group full of hope. While this is good, and provides the therapist with a powerful tool for work, members' expectations are often unreasonably and unrealistically high. This is particularly true for survivors who are new to therapy or new to group therapy, and believe the group will be the cure-all miracle therapy, which they have been waiting for.

The group does not produce dramatic changes in members. The changes that occur are subtle and incremental. Given the discrepancy between members' expectations and the reality of the group, it is vital that the therapist address this issue early and directly. In addition to discussing members' expectations in the pregroup interview, the therapist needs to address it again in the first session, when she or he is providing a general orientation to the group. The therapist should prepare members for possible feelings of disillusionment and frustration which may occur later in the group, when their early hopes are not realized.

CONTROLLED SELF-DISCLOSURE

Members' self-disclosures are critical to beginning the work of the group since they reduce anxieties and foster a sense of commonality. It would be unrealistic, however, to expect that members could provide detailed accounts either of their victimization or of other resulting problems.

Some members can be dramatically frank even in the first session but the majority of members remain understandably reluctant to reveal too much too soon. While survivors need to be encouraged to risk sharing with others, they also need to have permission to take their time doing so. Even as the therapist credits a member who reveals a great deal early on, she or he also tells others they are entitled to hold back what they don't yet feel ready to share.

The therapist must achieve a very delicate balance. On one hand, clients should not feel pressured to reveal sensitive information before they feel they are ready. On the other hand, if the therapist leaves this completely up to members, they may never feel ready. The therapist needs to firmly and repeatedly encourage members to be frank with each other, but ultimately must respect their wishes in this regard.

The therapist's insistence on honest discussion often results in members saying more than they had planned. Even though some members may be afraid to share something with the group, when they have finally done so, they inevitably are met with support, understanding, and acceptance. Some revelations may produce reactions of shock and revulsion, but these responses are not directed at the survivor who made the disclosure. Reactions, even those of disgust, act as a powerful source of affirmation and validation for the survivor.

Kevin Describes His Abuse

When Kevin first introduced himself to the group, he simply told them that he had been abused by his uncle from the time that he was 12 until he ran away at age 18. He described the abuse as "nasty," and said he'd save the "gory details" for later. Several sessions passed, and while Kevin was an active participant in discussion, he continued to avoid being more specific about his abuse, despite encouragement from the therapist and other members.

In the fifth session, members were talking about their deep sense of humiliation regarding their abuse, and their intense shame. The therapist again turned to Kevin, saying, "I suspect that this is an issue that touches you deeply, as you've described yourself as a gross and disgusting monster. The abuse left you feeling dirty and despicable."

Kevin responded, "I know where you want me to go with this. You want me to tell what happened to me, don't you?" The therapist said, "I think you are convinced they will be revolted by what you have to say. I know they won't, but you won't know that until you try."

Kevin took a deep breath and then proceeded to provide a graphic description of his abuse. As he talked, he became increasingly nervous. Initially, his uncle seduced him in the shower, and Kevin reported this "actually felt kind of good." The abuse continued to become more violent, sadistic, and involved several men. Kevin was also sodomized with large objects. He was forced to perform oral sex when the men had fecal matter on their penises. He was tied up and whipped, given enemas and forced to hold his bowel movements, urinated on, and pricked with needles on his genitals.

The group was visibly shaken, some were crying, and others were acutely agitated or angry. As the therapist processed this with members, it was clear the other members felt intense and profound sadness for Kevin and most expressed extreme anger toward his abusers. One member even commented that she would "gladly castrate the sons of bitches."

Kevin's abuse was sadistic and cruel. The group responded with understandable revulsion as well as sadness and anger. They were not repulsed by Kevin, but by what had happened to him. This reaction, like members' sorrow and rage, was helpful to Kevin. For years, he had minimized the severity of his abuse in an attempt to manage his feelings. His abuse was terrible and his recovery hinged on acknowledging it as well as the acute feelings of rage, sadness, and self-loathing that resulted from it. Even though Kevin was reluctant to share this information with the group, he had to if he was to get the kind of validation and affirmation he desperately needed.

Kevin's own reactions to his disclosures and to the group members' responses to him were typical of clients in his situation. Talking frankly about his abuse prompted powerful feelings of rage and despair, emotions that had been long suppressed and denied. Kevin also reported feeling "relieved" and "in a way, glad" that others in the group now knew about what happened to him. In response to a question, Kevin also reported that he believed that members were not upset with him, although he had a hard time understanding why the others in the group were getting angry at his uncle and his uncle's friends. While Kevin was able to let his defenses down enough to reveal a great deal about his abuse, these eventually resurfaced in his deep-seated mistrust and tendency to distance himself from others.

Members usually limit what they disclose in the early sessions and they need the help and support of the therapist to share more. The therapist should expect the first sessions to be characterized by controlled revelations, but must also encourage members to take greater risks in this area backed by the knowledge the therapist has gleaned from the pregroup interviews.

THE "EVERYONE-BUT-ME" PHENOMENON

An interesting dynamic apparent in the early sessions of the group, even as members begin to self-disclose and receive validation and support from others, is the continued belief that they are bad, unworthy, and responsible for their victimization. Most believe that all others in the group are true victims, worthy of the care and concern of others, but they somehow are different. They were unlovable or unworthy enough to have caused their abuse. Members are far more accepting of others than they are of themselves.

For example, Mike was struggling with strong feelings of guilt regarding his anger toward his ailing, elderly mother. Then Carol talked about her anger toward her mother, who, like Mike's mother, had been emotionally and physically neglectful, contributing directly to the sexual abuse through her lack of care, concern, and appropriate supervision. Mike, validating Carol's anger, said her mother didn't deserve anything but her contempt and her rage. When it was suggested to Mike that his situation was similar, he responded, "Things were different. Maybe my mother's indifference towards me was just because I didn't try hard enough to be a good son."

The sense of shame, responsibility, and worthlessness are chronic feelings that protect the survivor from the more painful realization of betrayal. Admitting betrayal generates intense feelings of rage and despair. While group members derive a tremendous amount of support and validation from others' disclosures and reactions to their own revelations, they nonetheless continue to hold on to the beliefs of their own intrinsic worthlessness. To consider the alternative — that they were not at fault — is even more threatening. Recovery depends upon a willingness to accept their own vulnerability, the injustice done to them, and feelings resulting from these realizations. While this alone will not alter a lifetime of guilt and shame, without the therapist's assistance, it is unlikely that members will be able to let go of these deeply felt views of themselves.

At every opportunity the therapist needs to point out any discrepancy between a members' view of themselves and the views they hold of another group member. The therapist assists members in seeing the protective function served by the everyone-but-me perspective. Even in the early weeks of the group, the therapist must begin to move members into feelings of despair and rage that lie beneath their sense of responsibility.

Andrew Begins to Face His Illusions

Andrew was noticeably empathetic and supportive of others in the group. As members disclosed their abuse or other painful aspects of their lives, he was always quick to note that the abusive individuals were "bastards" and "sick."

Andrew who was from a dysfunctional alcoholic family, had been abused by several men. He remembers no familial affection of any kind, describes himself as "the little man" in the family, who took care of everyone else. Andrew realized at a very young age that "no one in the whole world" cared about him.

In the fifth session, several members discussed their feelings of responsibility for the abuse. Jane said, "I know in my head I couldn't have caused this, but in my heart, where it counts, I feel like it must have been me, something I did."

"No, you're right," Andrew responded. "Your uncles were sick. How could you have caused your abuse? You were eight years old, for christ's sake. Eight-year-old kids don't ask to be f---ed!"

The therapist commented on Andrew's anger, noting Andrew's response was surprising since he blamed himself for his own victimization. She asked why Andrew viewed his abuse as different. Andrew said, "It just is. I was older. I should have known better. I know my family was f---ed up, but that doesn't make what I did right. My parents were alcoholics. How could I have expected them to care for me properly?"

"I know this may anger you," the therapist responded, "but I'll say it anyway. You did not deserve to be abused. You should not have been parenting your parents. You had a right to be loved, cared for, nurtured. I think you're afraid to accept these things. If you accept what I'm saying is true, you'll have to acknowledge how unfair it all was, how wrong your family was, how cruel your abusers were. Then, you'll have to start feeling the anger you try so hard to repress and deny. You'll also have to start feeling that despair I sense is just below the surface."

Andrew was thoughtful. "I need my illusions," he said. "I want a mother. I want to be hugged. Can you imagine how it feels to never have been hugged or even touched by your mother? I'm almost 50 years old and I still need to believe that my mother will be my mother. That if I just try a little harder, say the right thing, do the right thing, she'll love me."

Several members began crying, and Andrew became tearful as well. The therapist said, "I know this is tough, Andrew. But the truth is, I'm afraid you'll never get what you want from your family. Never. And you're paying such a high price for your illusions — your sense of worth and esteem."

While understanding Andrew's perspective, in this instance the therapist felt compelled to challenge it. His despair was acute, and his anger frightening to him. However, it was important for him to begin to acknowledge these feelings if he was ever going to develop a sense of himself as a valuable, lovable individual.

FOCUS ON CONTENT

The early phase is dominated by a focus on content, as opposed to process issues. The therapist, however, can use this time to begin to develop members' sensitivity to the ways they work together and relate to each other.

A therapy group with a focus on the here and now has the potential of being particularly beneficial to its members. Such a focus develops over time, however. Commenting on feelings and dynamics between individuals as these occur is a new and threatening experience for survivors. As members become acquainted with each other, the focus necessarily begins with the past, and with events and people that exist outside the group's boundaries. Although anxiety surrounds members' disclosures, honest discussion regarding members' feelings about each other provokes even greater concern.

In the first session as the therapist explains the value of the group, she or he can point out the value of the here and now. Members' reactions to each other mirror their reactions to people outside the group. The difference between the group and the world outside is that, in group, members can process their reactions immediately and come to a better understanding of themselves and the way they relate to others.

As members begin relating to each other, the therapist can explore their immediate responses using traditional techniques such as identifying and articulating emotions members feel toward each other. At the beginning of each session as part of the previous sessions' review, the therapist can comment on the way the group is working, asking members for their input. The therapist should share his or her own immediate reactions and feelings towards the group as these happen. The therapist can increasingly request the group to be self-reflective, by asking questions such as, "What's going on with you now?"

The early sessions inevitably set the stage and tone for the later work of the group. This is no more apparent than in the therapist's handling of the here and now. As difficult as it is for members to begin talking honestly about their victimization with each other, this is actually easier and less threatening to them than talking to each other about each other. The therapist must, through modeling and through demands made on members, encourage them to explore their immediate, spontaneous responses to each other.

As members become more secure and comfortable with each other, their interpersonal difficulties become more apparent and provide the therapist with a valuable opportunity to further the work of the group. If members are required to explore their reactions as these occur, it is easier if members have been helped to be self-reflective from the beginning.

5
The Middle Phase

There is no precise moment when the group moves from the beginning to the middle, or work, phase. Gradually but perceptibly, however, group dynamics begin to shift, typically around the fifth or sixth session. As the comfort level increases, members are freed from the anxieties and worries troubling them at the outset. Early themes are replaced by dynamics reflecting members' attempts to deal with their own abuse and with each other.

Several themes that emerge in the middle phase reveal how difficult and frightening the group's work is for members. The theme that predominates is the expression and management of intense feelings of rage and loss. The tendency for members to dissociate during particularly difficult sessions and a growing disenchantment with the group which prompts some members to contemplate quitting are two other important dynamics. These latter two themes may be viewed as manifestations of members' fears about where the group is taking them and their attempts at coping with these anxieties.

The group's work in the middle phase is predicated upon the climate created in the beginning. Further, the lasting therapeutic benefits of the group depend — to some extent — upon the group's ability to terminate. A true therapy group works from the first session through the last. What changes in the duration of the group is the nature and focus of this work.

EXPRESSING RAGE AND LOSS

No case example can accurately portray the powerful dynamic of survivors expressing feelings of rage and loss which have been suppressed and denied for years. The intensity and depth of these feelings are so overwhelming, survivors often go to great lengths to deny their existence. These feelings, coupled with members' attempts to manage them, explain some of their more troublesome struggles as adults.

Bob Reacts to Jennifer's Disclosure

In the eighth session, Jennifer disclosed to the group that her 26-year-old daughter had also been sexually abused when she was a child. At the time it happened, Jennifer had no idea, but as her daughter grew into adulthood and Jennifer became healthier and more aware, she began to suspect something was wrong. Jennifer reported that, until now, she had not been willing to deal with it or talk about it.

Jennifer described her feelings about her daughter's abuse, particularly her profound sense of responsibility and guilt. When Jennifer began crying, so did Janet, whose own daughter had been sexually molested. The group's mood changed to deep sadness. Jennifer's and Janet's feelings regarding their daughters revived so many feelings about their own abuse. The other two women in the group also became teary-eyed, and one commented that even though she believed her daughter hadn't been victimized, she "just felt so sad and lost."

While Bob sat quietly, he was clearly agitated and upset. When prompted, Bob admitted he "felt like he just had to get up and get out of the room because the walls were closing in."

When questioned, Bob responded, "I know that this will sound weird, but as I'm listening to everyone, what I'm thinking is how lucky Janet's and Jennifer's daughters are. Not because they were abused, but because their mothers cared enough to be upset. When I told my mother about my abuse, all she could say is, 'Why didn't you tell me?' She then went back to watching the television show. All I've ever wanted was for someone to love me, hold me, touch me. What's so wrong with me that my mother doesn't love me?"

Bob then became teary-eyed but initially denied it. Susan, who had been listening intently, said, "Bob, go ahead, it's okay. You may be 45 years old, but inside you're still a little boy who's really sad and wants a mom. Go ahead and cry. We won't think you're weird."

This was Bob's second group experience and, while he always displayed an air of sadness, he was adamant about not wanting to explore these feelings. He freely acknowledged that if he gave in to his feelings, he'd have to admit to himself that his mother and father were not there for him when he was a child and would never be there for him as an adult. He also admitted that he grew up thinking "tears were for sissies," which made it was doubly difficult for Bob to explore his grief.

Jennifer's sadness, coupled with that of the other women in the group, triggered many of Bob's deepest feelings of despair about his abuse. The honest expression of Jennifer's and Janet's emotion helped Bob to get in touch with his feelings and express them. The female members' open displays of sadness were powerful sources of validation for Bob's own feelings. Susan's reassurance that crying was okay and her characterization of Bob as a "little boy" were not only accurate, they paved the way for Bob's eventual expression of sadness.

The mixed-sex group structure, where both men and women act out different styles of managing feelings, stimulates discussions of grief, rage, and sadness. The more comfortable members are with each other, the more able they are to reveal the most sensitive and harmful aspects of their abuse and their lives. As these disclosures become more frank, they often prompt deeply felt, long-suppressed feelings in both the member who expresses the disclosure and those who listen to it.

Janet's Rape Disclosure

In the eighth session, members had been discussing their feelings of betrayal and anger toward individuals who did not protect them when Janet began to talk in depth about her abuse. To this point, her disclosures, while frank, had been incomplete.

While Janet had previously revealed she was repeatedly molested by her three brothers, this time she reported that when she was about nine or 10, she was raped by a group of boys while her older brother looked on. This particular incident was preceded by what she now understood to be her brother lying to her in order to get her into an abandoned house, where the rape took place. Janet began to cry softly and continued with the memory of her brother laughing as his friends "took turns with her." She remembered how humiliated and ashamed she felt then — feelings that never left.

When Janet began sobbing uncontrollably, several other group members became teary-eyed or cried, including two of the men. Janet ended by remembering, when she was about six or seven, wanting "some stupid candles that looked like turkeys." With great difficulty, she disclosed that after her oldest brother raped her, he gave her the candles as a "present for keeping their secret."

Reading this example can not adequately convey Janet's grief and the impact her pain had on the group. For at least five minutes following her final comments, she wept uncontrollably. Three other members also cried freely. All were deeply affected by her disclosure. The depth of Janet's sense of betrayal was overwhelming, as was her sense of shame and grief.

While Janet had been in therapy for several years, she had only recently been able to acknowledge her grief. Until she began to talk about these two experiences, Janet had not realized how deep and intense her feelings of shame and humiliation were. Janet admitted that for years she had been afraid of crying about her abuse because if she "started, I thought I'd never be able to stop"— a sentiment frequently heard from both men and women.

Fear of Expressing Rage and Sadness

Expressing sadness inevitably triggers anger aimed at both the injustice and those responsible for it. Members' feelings of rage are typically accompanied by grief at what they have lost.

As frightening as it seems to survivors, it often is easier to deal with anger than with sadness. As one member of the group noted, "I can get angry easy. My parents were incapable of loving me and because of their selfishness and warped personalities, they let me get abused. I can't be sad, because if I do, I'll really have to accept, once and for all, that I didn't come from the Cleaver family and that I will never, ever have a mother or father to love me. I can't accept that yet. I still yearn for it, I still want it."

Many survivors are also terrified of their anger, convinced that if they start to experience their rage, they will destroy themselves and others. This fear combined with the intensity of the rage was described by a female group member, who stated, "Most of the time, I just won't deal with anger. But then something will trigger it, usually something my husband does. Then I could kill him. I mean I could kill him with my bare hands. I think of all kinds of ways to torture him, to make him hurt like I've been hurt. It makes me feel crazy, out of control. I believe I could kill him and myself, too."

Learning to Manage Feelings

The therapist has the challenging, at times, overwhelming task of helping members express and manage these feelings. To some extent, the therapist's actions are consistent with already identified behaviors. The group therapist's ability to articulate the client's feelings is critical. Members must be helped to express painful feelings which usually involves the therapist drawing attention to emerging feelings, even if the survivor is not yet aware of them. The therapist needs to rely upon members' facial expressions, tone of voice, and other non-verbal behaviors, as well as knowledge of an individual's experiences and common abuse reactions.

Survivors' fears about losing control can be so strong as to completely block their own or the therapist's efforts to get in touch with feelings which have been suppressed for a long time. Many survivors grew up in families where feelings of sorrow or anger were either denied or were expressed inappropriately.

In order for the therapist to properly address members' fears about expressing rage or despair, members need to be reassured that they, the group, and the therapist will survive the experience. The therapist may need to frequently reiterate to members that she or he is not afraid of them or for them, and assure them that she or he will not let them get out of control, hurt themselves or anyone else in the group. Members must explore and vent their feelings of rage and sadness, and survive the experience. Only then can they start to accept and come to terms with their emotions. The more members express these feelings, the less frightening and more manageable they become.

The therapist must provide ways of venting feelings, for example, by telling clients to "beat the floor," "pound the sofa," or urging members to "turn away and cry," if that is easier for them. She or he also can discuss in group what members can do when they leave, both to stimulate the expression of feelings and to make these feelings more manageable to them.

Peter explained he would take a picture of his abuser and, with a baseball bat, strike it repeatedly with all his might. Prompted by this suggestion, several other members tried it. Similarly, members can be encouraged to scream as loudly as they can into a pillow or in the shower. The therapist may also suggest clients look at photographs of themselves as children and experience the inevitable sadness this evokes. Group members may be encouraged to bring these photographs into group. This triggers intense and profound discussions of sadness.

Survivors' abilities to utilize these suggestions vary widely. Some, particularly those who have been in therapy for some time, are able to risk a great deal, both within and outside of the group, venting powerful and deep feelings of grief and rage. Without the therapist's guidance, reassurance, and persistence, however, it is unlikely they would have the courage to engage in this process. Further, the support, acceptance, and validation of the group is crucial, as are the expressions of similar feelings by other members.

For those relatively new to therapy, the expression of such feelings remains frightening and alien. While they may not yet be ready to explore in depth their rage and despair, observing others going through and surviving this process is beneficial.

Losing Control

The questions most frequently asked by therapists have to do with members losing control. "What happens if someone really goes off the deep end? What do I do?" The expression of profound, raw feelings typically does not precipitate decompensation among members. While to some extent, this reflects the criteria used to determine group membership, it also shows that survivors are stronger than they (and their therapists) often think. However, the therapist must take threats of harm to self or others seriously and be prepared to act accordingly.

While the therapist pays attention to the member who is venting powerful feelings, he or she observes the reactions of other group members at the same time. This, too, is a concern of therapists. "How do you handle other members of the group? Aren't they upset? What if they lose control?"

As one member speaks, the therapist should consistently monitor the group's reactions to assess whether the individual member's disclosures are prompting similar feelings in others. As one member expresses intense feelings, others in the group generally respond with anxiety, fear, and concern, reactions which stem from several sources. Members are frightened by the feelings evoked by someone else's disclosure. Members feel ill-equipped to help their fellow member, they don't know what to say or how to show support. This sense of powerlessness often leads to feelings of guilt and is consistent with survivors' own sense of worthlessness and inadequacy. Members are uncomfortable in the presence of someone who is expressing such raw, naked emotions. As it is for most individuals, the sight of someone else in deep distress is disconcerting and unsettling.

It is important for the group to tolerate the expression of rage and sadness. A member may attempt to sabotage this process by changing the subject and in other ways seeking to divert the focus of the group. Whenever possible, the therapist should point out this dynamic, why it is happening, and turn the group's focus once again back to the member in distress. Clearly, the therapist's influence is limited in this regard. If individual members or the group as a whole are not ready for such intense displays, the group and the individual's attentions continue to be diverted, no matter what the therapist does.

Processing Intense Emotional Reactions

The more mature the group, the better able it will be to tolerate the distress of members. Typically, members sit quietly and listen intently as another is speaking. If one individual begins crying, others may start to cry. Some may clench or pound their fists as another individual expresses anger. When the individual is finished, the therapist must process the experience. Appropriate questions include, "How are you feeling?" "Do you need to say anything else?" and "Are you okay?" (to the individual member) and "What was this like for the rest of you?"

The therapist assesses how the individual member is doing and credits the member for being honest and able to take risks. Then the therapist must ascertain what, if anything, the individual would have wanted from the group as she or he was experiencing pain, and what, if anything, she or he wants from them now. Individual members are likely to respond they need to be left alone or they do not want anyone to try to comfort or hold them while they are upset. This is instructive to everyone and diminishes members' sense of helplessness.

It is important for the group to share a member's reactions, concern, sense of helplessness, and fears as well as to reassure and help the individual learn they feel similar emotions. While members might be afraid of what the individual's revelations might do to them, when the individual hears from others in the group they were not frightened of him or her, this lessens the member's fears about himself or herself.

Among the therapist's greatest dilemmas in leading a group for survivors is reacting and responding to expressions of rage and sadness — feelings which may deeply affect the therapist. While the therapist may be moved to respond with reassuring comments and gestures to individual members, this may be ill advised. Survivors need to learn how to give and receive support and if the therapist provides the comfort and reassurance, others in the group are deprived of the opportunity to do this. Premature displays of physical support and comfort may cut short the individual's expressions of rage and sorrow. The therapist, like the members, may have to learn to tolerate the despair of others and to monitor the temptation to jump in too quickly.

Less mature groups may need the therapist's support in responding to the distress of another member. Modeling appropriate behavior is vital and the therapist must keep the ultimate goal in mind: to pave the way for members to take over this task.

Research exploring the expression and management of intense feelings in therapy groups is scant. One study found that intense emotional affect resulting from the expression of both negative, or confrontive, and positive feelings in group is beneficial if this occurs in a safe context and if members ultimately experience a reduction in the intensity of their feelings (Bell et al. 1989). There also is some evidence to suggest that groups where members become aware of their feelings, particularly of anger and loneliness, are helpful.

INCREASE IN FLASHBACKS AND EMERGENCE OF NEW MEMORIES

As members' disclosures become more frank, and as significant feelings are more freely expressed, many in the group begin to experience flashbacks and resurging memories. While survivors do not need to recall all aspects of their victimization or their lost childhoods in order to successfully recover, material that surfaces more or less spontaneously should be viewed as a positive step. While the therapist may not deliberately use the group to stimulate the return of memories in individual members, this does occur quite frequently and must be dealt with.

Lost memories are significant and usually painful. While a newly remembered experience has long been hidden from the member's consciousness, it has nonetheless been an influential force in shaping his or her behavior.

Janet Remembers

In one particular survivors' group, there had been much discussion of sadness, humiliation, and shame. The tone of these groups, coupled with the progress Janet was making in therapy precipitated the return of some very painful memories. As noted in an earlier example, she had always known that her brothers had molested her and she also had a dim awareness that other boys were involved.

Janet's tearful memory of her brother "setting her up" to be raped by his friends had been recently remembered. Janet's memory of the candles her brother used to "buy" her silence with was also new, although she knew she had an aversion to Thanksgiving decorations but never understood why. These experiences, repressed for years, left Janet feeling ashamed, betrayed, and humiliated. Like pieces of a puzzle, these memories helped Janet to connect her feelings to tangible experiences and process her reactions.

In many instances, the member does not experience complete recall of an event, but rather begins to have the sensation that "something else is coming."

Peter Suspects More Abuse

Peter reported he was increasingly having the sense that there was more to his abuse than he recalled. He clearly remembered being sodomized by an older brother, but he reported he had a gut feeling someone else abused him. He said he could almost see the face of a man but then it faded. This client also told the group he realized whenever he got into a shower he "zoned out"— he had no memory of taking a shower at all. He concluded, probably correctly, he must have been assaulted in a shower or bathroom, even though he had yet to recall the specific incident.

Members, often completely unexpectedly, find themselves re-experiencing their childhoods — places and situations — where they were abused. The issue is not one of the spontaneous retrieval of a lost memory. The individual feels as if he or she is "back there."

Bob's Retrieval of the Past

As one member was talking in detail about her abuse, Bob seemed distant. Initially, he appeared not to hear a question asked of him. But when asked again, he reported at that moment he was 10 years old again and back in the neighborhood where he grew up and where he was abused. He went on to describe how real this felt to him, that he could "almost see the sights, smell the scents, and hear the sounds of his childhood."

Sally Remembers

Sally reported to the group she was driving down the street when she passed a house similar to the one which she had grown up in. "All of a sudden I was six again," she said. "My heart was beating so fast. I was so afraid, paralyzed — just like I used to be when I knew my uncles and cousins [her abusers] were around."

Dealing with Memories and Flashbacks

The retrieval of new memories and flashbacks are disconcerting and frightening to survivors. For many they are disheartening. The return of memories and flashbacks are inevitable aspects of group treatment for survivors, and it is the group's work which results in these very disconcerting experiences for these individuals.

As Bob put it, "Just when I thought I was getting things together, beginning to make sense out of my past, along comes this new memory. Now I've got to deal with the fact that I wasn't just assaulted individually by these guys, but that they raped me together. Now I know I was gang raped."

In the pregroup interview, the therapist should prepare clients for the possibility that new memories will return or that they will experience flashbacks. The therapist can explain why these experiences occur, as well as their therapeutic implications. Since new memories and flashbacks and their impact remain highly abstract to the survivor at this point, the therapist should also consider exploring with the client in the pregroup session whether he or she has ever experienced such phenomena, and if so, how this felt.

Group Support

When the group commences, the therapist once again reminds members that as the group progresses and as members' revelations become more frank and painful, they may experience new memories, flashbacks, and nightmares. The therapist should urge members to talk about these events, should they occur, within the group. Members usually do want to talk about these issues in group, largely because they are so confused and frightened by them. Many survivors have had these experiences, either spontaneously or as an outgrowth of therapy, and, not surprisingly, the most potent and powerful source of support comes from others in the group.

The most important consideration is helping survivors to tolerate these experiences. This is best accomplished by preparing members for the possibility these reactions may occur, helping survivors to understand their meaning, and facilitating members' support and comfort to each other. Members become aware of the missing links in their lives, and with the therapist's and group's assistance, they can grow from these experiences.

The Accuracy of Memories

Debate surrounds the accuracy of memories retrieved by survivors in therapy. It has been argued that such memories may be artifacts of the therapy, not a reflection of clients' actual experiences. In the case of groups for survivors, it also has been asserted that recollections which occur during the group may reflect over identification among members and an excessive need to conform (Mayer 1995).

It is certainly the case that returning memories during the group are triggered, and often colored, by others' recollections. The possibility that memories which return to members during the group are false should, of course, be considered by the therapist and addressed directly in the group, if necessary. The culture of the group should not require the emergence of new memories, but rather should accept this phenomenon and provide support to members who experience it.

Typically, memories return spontaneously with little or no specific prodding from the therapist or the other members of the group. In many instances, in fact, memories return *despite* the member's efforts to prevent this from happening. The recalled experiences may be quite different from those which have been revealed by others in the group.

DISILLUSIONMENT WITH THE GROUP

As the work of the group becomes more intense, members' reservations about their participation often are heightened. Even though members find the group comforting and look to it as a source of support and connection to others, they also are frightened by what it is doing to them. Experiencing painful and overwhelming feelings, subjected to new memories and flashbacks, witnessing others' despair and anger, a common and

understandable question becomes, "Is this worth it?" Feelings
of disillusionment may be powerful and prompt some to
contemplate quitting. While withdrawing from the group may
be an appropriate option in a few cases, in most instances
members need to be helped to articulate their concerns and
encouraged to continue.

Carol Decides to Quit the Group

As the group progressed into its sixth week, Carol
had become increasingly quiet. While Carol
acknowledged in group that she was "having some
problems," she was reluctant to elaborate.

Carol called the therapist the day before the seventh
session and admitted she was thinking of quitting, that she
"just didn't feel the group was right for her at this time."
Carol explained she was still very much trying to deal
with the recent suicide of her son, Joe, 10 months before,
and she did not feel the group could help her with this.

While she knew that Carol was still having a difficult
time dealing with her son's death, the therapist wondered
if this was an excuse for Carol to leave. "In one sense you
are right," the therapist told her. "This is not a group for
people who are dealing with the death of a loved one.
However, this is a group that has been dealing with grief,
sadness, and guilt, and these are all feelings that you seem
to be having great difficulty with. My sense is that your
guilt and shame over your abuse has been heightened and
intensified as a result of Joe's death. I don't want to
minimize your grief over his death, but I can't help but see
the connection to your feelings about you and your abuse.
And these are feelings that everyone in the group relates
to. I wonder whether, at some level, you're afraid to share
your grief with the group, afraid of letting it go. There

have already been many tears in this group, and I wonder if that's frightening to you."

"I don't know," Carol responded. "What you say makes sense. I know that I feel awful, that I need to talk about this stuff, but I'm so sad. It's so hard."

When asked if she would be willing to talk about her concerns in the next group, Carol agreed. In the following session, Carol was able to talk about her reservations in continuing with the group, her sorrow about her son, specifically, and her childhood, generally. Her revelations prompted others to express deep sadness and grief. She received strong support and understanding from the others.

Peter commented, "I may not have lost a son, but I think I can appreciate how awful you must feel. I want you to know you can talk about it here. You need to talk about this, and I hope you feel you can talk to us."

Carol's reservations about the group stemmed from her reluctance to discuss her grief and sense of responsibility for the death of her son. To some extent she made a legitimate point. While the group was for survivors of sexual abuse, not for survivors of suicide, this excuse provided her with a reasonably sounding rationale to quit. When Carol brought up her concerns with the group, they, like the therapist, encouraged her to share her pain and conveyed an understanding of her reluctance.

Carol decided to remain in the group. If left to her own devices, she probably would have quit and remained convinced that she had made the right decision. The support and understanding of the group provided Carol with the motivation and encouragement she needed to continue, to risk being honest in the group concerning her son's death and the powerful sense of responsibility she was feeling.

Anticipating Disillusionment

The therapist should anticipate disillusionment among some of the group's members and be prepared to assist them in managing these feelings. In both the pregroup interview and the first session, the therapist should discuss the possibility of group disenchantment with members. Clients should be urged to talk about these feelings when they occur, so that they can get the support and encouragement of others who have been through it. The more realistic survivors are when the enter group therapy, the less intense and more manageable their sense of disillusionment will be later on. This underscores the importance of helping clients to develop an accurate sense about what the group can and cannot do for them. The stronger members' feelings are during the "honeymoon" period in the beginning, the more likely it is that they will experience disillusionment later on in the work phase of the group.

The Therapist's Support System

A survivor's sense of disillusionment can be so strong as to lead the therapist to question the value and purpose of the group. Not only is it difficult for the therapist to watch members express feelings of despair and rage, but it is even more difficult to watch members leaving a group session feeling worse than when they came in. To be sure, over time, members do make progress. Change is slow, however, and most sessions end with members feeling spent, sad, or angry. In all likelihood, the therapist will need the advice, support, and encouragement of colleagues to manage his or her own feelings of ambivalence resulting from these powerful group dynamics.

DISSOCIATION DURING THE SESSION

Often occurring during particularly painful and intense discussions is the tendency of some or all members to dissociate. The most common pattern is for several members to dissociate during difficult periods in the group. Dissociation does not usually continue for the whole session and members more or less spontaneously "return" to the group sometime during the meeting.

A disconcerting dynamic for both therapist and member, it is helpful to prepare survivors beforehand for the possibility of dissociation during particularly painful or difficult sessions. In both the pregroup interview and the first session, the therapist should discuss this dynamic, its meaning, and urge clients to let her or him know if dissociation happens.

The Therapist Discovers Collective Dissociation

The therapist began the session by providing a review of the previous week's meeting. Noting the previous session had been a very painful one, the therapist related she cried on the way home. If she was upset by this last session, the therapist told the group, she "could imagine how the members of the group must have felt." Congratulating everyone for showing up for the session, the therapist observed, "Sometimes after a particularly difficult group, members are tempted to run away and not return."

Blank stares from everyone in the group prompted the therapist to inquire if members recalled the last session. Fred stated, "As you're talking, I'm starting to remember it. But to be honest, when you started talking, saying how sad you were after last week's session, I thought we must have attended different groups, since I came in here thinking that we hadn't done much last week. I was actually feeling kind of disappointed about our last meeting."

In processing details of the previous session, every member reported that they had either full or partial memory loss regarding the previous session. Most reported that they did not know "where they went" or what they were thinking, they just did not recall the group as exceptionally intense. Two members were able to report that they "took off for those places where they always went while they were being abused."

Monitoring Dissociation in the Group

When the group's focus becomes intense, the therapist needs to observe who stayed with the discussion and who dissociated. As the group matures and members become more aware both of themselves and each other, they become better able to monitor this dynamic on their own.

Members are entitled to their defenses and, while the group's focus may cause some members to dissociate, the therapist should avoid interrupting this process. In most cases, when the survivor is able to connect with the group and attend to its discussion, he or she will. Over time, and with the continued support of the therapist and others in the group, members are more able to tolerate intense exchanges and this behavior often becomes less frequent as the group progresses. Even so, during particularly powerful moments, one may expect that dissociation among most or even all members may result. When this phenomenon occurs, it is important for the therapist to point this out to the individual and the group, as well as discuss its meaning and significance. The therapist may wish to ask members who are particularly prone to this behavior if there is anything that could have been done to help them stay aware.

However, it is unlikely that these individuals will be able to offer any suggestions.

Dissociation is a strategy survivors have used, for the most part unconsciously, for years and is a coping mechanism to help them endure their abuse and survive. When the group's work becomes too intense, therefore, some members need to temporarily retreat. Both the therapist and members must tolerate this phenomenon and the therapist must help members recall the session and specifically pinpoint what led to the dissociative behavior. This underscores the value of sessional review and emphasizes the importance of helping the group focus on the here and now.

DISCUSSING SEXUALITY

The ability of the group to deal effectively with members' sexual experiences depends upon the therapist's own level of comfort. Survivors must come to terms not only with their childhood victimization but also with numerous other experiences in which they were sexually exploited. In some cases, survivors were raped by strangers, acquaintances, and partners. In other instances, they engaged in sexual behaviors causing them great shame, humiliation, and degradation. Others have been involved in homosexual relationships and have experienced feelings of guilt and confusion. Still others have participated in sadomasochistic sexual relationships in which they were injured.

Survivors' sense of adult sexuality is usually distorted, and their basic knowledge about sexual functioning is incomplete, at best, and erroneous, at worst. Many survivors have unrealistic views and are preoccupied with what constitutes normal sex. The therapist must be prepared not only to help members to discuss sensitive and embarrassing aspects of their sexuality, but also to assist them in developing a more realistic perspective on sexual functioning.

One of the most notable features of the group's focus on sex is the amount of energy members expend and the level of animation that exists as members interact with each other. Once the taboo against discussing sex has been lifted, members experience an enormous sense of relief, all jumping in at once.

Overcoming Shame

Survivors' deep-rooted sense of responsibility for their abuse is easier to remedy than the sense of shame and remorse about subsequent sexual experiences the survivor may have had. The comments of Denise illustrate this point. "Week after week, I come here and listen to you [the therapist] and everybody else," she told the group. "And I try to believe what you say, that I didn't seduce my father into abusing me. And I guess there is a small part of me that knows that, because I was a child, and children can't do that. But my being a prostitute is a different thing altogether. I was older, an adult. I willingly went with men, did things with them that were dirty and cheap. I accepted their money and kept on doing it. How can I believe anything other than I'm cheap — a slut, a whore?"

The only way such beliefs can be abandoned is for members to discuss their sexual experiences in an atmosphere of acceptance and understanding. When survivors reveal their sexual secrets and receive affirmation and validation, their sense of shame can be lessened.

The therapist must pave the way for members' sexual disclosures by bringing their concerns out into the open. Survivors' anxieties at first are expressed indirectly. Members often may wish to share their concerns with the therapist outside of the group. But the therapist must be prepared to acknowledge members' worries and help them share their concerns with the group directly. This reinforces the norm that whatever is shared with the therapist outside of the group must also be disclosed within the group.

George's Confession

After group, George asked if he could talk with the therapist alone, saying he was "really bothered by something." For several minutes, George anxiously attempted to talk but had great difficulty. "Whatever is bugging you," the therapist said, "you must feel like you want someone to know or else you wouldn't have asked me to stay after. I know you may not believe this, but I can't think of anything that you could tell me that would shock me or disgust me."

George proceeded hesitantly to talk about his worries concerning his sexual behavior. He revealed that he had not been with a woman for a long time. He found himself getting "horny," and doing "weird s---." He said he would often masturbate while inserting the handle of a hair brush into his anus. While he stated this did not feel good and he felt ashamed, he said, "Somehow, I just feel like I have to do it, like I deserve to be screwed."

When asked if there was anything else he needed to share with her, George said, "No." The therapist credited George for being so honest and assured him that she was not shocked by what he had told her. The therapist briefly explained that George's behavior might reflect his feelings of self-disgust and urged George to talk about this with his individual therapist. She also encouraged him to discuss his behavior and his feelings with the group.

While George expressed fear about discussing his concerns in the group, the therapist responded, "I can't help but think that at some level you must want the group to know, or else you wouldn't have talked to me." George agreed, but said, "I know they will really think I'm warped."

In the session that followed, the therapist provided a review of the previous week's group. She then told members that George had talked with her and had something he needed to share with them. With only a little prodding, George disclosed his secret to the group. Members' responses were swift. Several related previously undisclosed aspects of their own sex lives. One woman revealed that she "could only do it and have an orgasm" if she was afraid or if she was being physically hurt. Another man reported, "Things are so bad with me now that I can't even get it up anymore. My girlfriend wants to have sex, and I just can't. I can't get an erection."

Without assistance from the therapist, members were also able to tell George how much they appreciated him talking about his concerns, since it opened up a discussion that they wanted but were afraid to initiate. All expressed support and understanding of George's feelings. Members were able to help George see that his desire to sodomize himself was closely linked to his anger. Not only was it a reflection of his sense of shame and guilt over his abuse, it also surfaced most strongly when he got angry at others, particularly those at work.

George harbored intense feelings of embarrassment, shame, and bewilderment regarding his sexual behavior. As difficult and painful as it was for him to share his concerns with the group, the resulting support and validation he received were extremely therapeutic. Because of his courage, members assured George, a necessary discussion — one they needed to have — took place.

George's revelations stimulated the disclosures of others, and the tone for the remainder of this meeting was, as one of the members described it, about "true confessions." Nearly all members shared a "dirty secret" about their sexual activity as adults. The benefit of these disclosures was that, as with George, members were met with understanding and support. No one was ridiculed, no one was made to feel dirty or disgusting.

Connecting Childhood to Adult Behavior

Many survivors benefit from developing an understanding of the connection between their sexual behavior as adults and their exploitation as children. In general, survivors' adult sexual behavior tends to mirror and replay their victimization as children and feelings of self-disgust and self-loathing. Achieving an understanding of this connection can be particularly helpful in reducing the sense of guilt and confusion survivors have concerning their adult sexual behavior.

The therapist may provide interpretations of members' experiences, pointing out that their sexual activities continue to reinforce and perpetuate their negative self-definitions. The more mature the group, the better able the members are to do this themselves. As in the case with George, it was another male in the group who helped George realize that his desire to sodomize himself was often stimulated by his anger — turned inwardly against himself. Such a realization is particularly powerful and helpful if it has been prompted by other members in the group.

Accepting Responsibility

While it is important for survivors to understand the context of their adult sexual behavior, they also must come to terms with their actions and accept responsibility for their behaviors. The therapist needs to help members understand why they may have engaged in sexual behaviors causing them shame and embarrassment. They must also be helped, in many cases, to accept responsibility for their actions.

For example, numbers of group members, both male and female, have engaged in prostitution. It is not enough for these individuals to understand that their involvement in this activity reflected their feelings of self-disgust, a desire to be in control, and to use others as they had been used. In order for members to truly come to terms with their experiences they must acknowledge their responsibility. As Denise commented, "The truth of the matter is, I took the money, I solicited sex. No one forced me to. I'm not proud of it but it's a part of my past that I have to accept if I'm going to get past this stuff." The therapist has an obligation to help members understand that while a sense of blame may not be warranted, if they are to successfully recover, ownership of their behavior is necessary.

Developing a Realistic View
of Sexual Functioning

Survivors typically need to develop a more realistic perspective regarding adult sexual functioning. The therapist has the additional responsibility of assisting members in this endeavor. "What is normal sex?" is one of the questions members most frequently ask. Given their dysfunctional introduction to sexuality, this concern is understandable. Most survivors have no conception of what it means to be in a healthy, satisfying sexual relationship.

Members must become familiar and comfortable with their own bodies and with their own sexuality. Frank discussions of masturbation and achieving orgasms, while extremely helpful, often are not sufficient to resolve members' concerns. Perhaps more than other topics that surface in group, members often need the assistance of an individual therapist to deal successfully with their sexual dysfunction.

Members may ask, usually indirectly and subtly, about the therapist's sexual relationships. Such questions typically reflect members' concerns with normalcy. While the therapist's use of self in working with survivors is valuable and, at times, necessary, in this case it is advisable to refrain from providing personal information. Too much disclosure in this area would be inappropriate and could be sexually stimulating to some members. While members may think they want to know about their therapist's sex life, what they really are interested in and need to know about is what a healthy, adult sexual relationship is like.

In mature groups, the discussion may evolve into one that may be best characterized as men and women trying to come to terms with an off-limits subject. The discussion becomes less focused on members' abuse and the sexual impact, and more concerned with developing comfort and learning how to experience joy in their sexuality.

FOCUSING ON THE HERE AND NOW

As members' comfort with each other increases, so, too, does their ability to concentrate on here-and-now interactions. Since this is such a difficult and alien behavior, the therapist must, from the outset, help members process their reactions to each other as they occur. The group's ability to deal with the immediate present is contingent upon the therapist's actions in the beginning phase. It is unrealistic to expect members to engage in this self-reflection without the direction and guidance of the group therapist. The group's ability to focus on the immediate present does not appear spontaneously, it develops gradually.

Members' abilities to deal with their here-and-now reactions with each other are heavily dependent upon the therapist's skill and the climate she or he creates. Even as members become better able to monitor and reflect on their interactions, they continue to require the encouragement and support of the therapist, who must continue to monitor members' reactions to each other and assist members in identifying these as they occur.

One of the more important here-and-now themes is evidenced as anger between members. The earliest manifestations of this dynamic reflect members' distorted perceptions of each other.

Bob Misunderstands Denise's Behavior

For much of the group, Denise had maintained a tough, hard exterior, daring anyone to try to "f--- with her." She had great difficulty acknowledging sadness about her abuse and often stated, "I don't have a mother or a father. As far as I'm concerned they're dead." Despite attempts to get her to explore her feelings of despair or fear, Denise remained stoic and superficially uncaring and angry.

In the past few sessions, Bob was becoming increasingly agitated and nervous whenever Denise would talk. Initially, when this was pointed out to him, he denied it. In the twelfth session, Denise was again commenting that she was never "going to get hurt again. No one will ever f--- with me again. I'm going to live my life as I see fit, f--- everybody else."

Bob would not look at Denise. He sat quietly, playing nervously with his hands. One of the women in the group said, "Come on, Bob, you look upset. What's up? Is it Denise?"

Reluctantly, Bob revealed that he was "furious" with Denise. "As soon as she opens her mouth, I get pissed at her," he said. "I'm sick of her bulls---! This 'I don't care' s--- gets on my nerves big time."

The initial reaction in the group was shock because such an outburst was uncharacteristic of Bob. One of the members suggested, however, that "Denise really stirred up something for you, didn't she? Who does she remind you of? Isn't that how you think of your mother, like she's cold and hard?"

The interesting aspect of this exchange was the interpretations of Bob's anger coming from the members themselves. Bob had talked quite often about his mother, who seemed to have been aloof, uncaring, and emotionally neglectful. However, he had rarely been able to express any anger at her.

Because this group was a mature, advanced group, the members processed this experience and their reactions to it. With little assistance, they were able to help Bob see how his anger at Denise was really a reflection of the rage he felt towards his mother, to help Denise process her sense of having been "picked on," and to understand their own reactions to Bob's outburst, including their own anger and confusion.

Conflicts and Disagreements

An inevitable aspect of a mature working group, like intimate relationships generally, is the presence of conflict and disagreement. A truly cohesive group is one where differences among members can be articulated. Just as members benefit from surviving their own and others' expressions of rage and pain, so, too, do all benefit from the emergence and successful resolution of disagreements.

Sources of conflict range from simple differences of opinion to concern over the behavior of another member. For example, in one group session a great deal of anger was prompted by Peter's decision to accept an invitation to talk to a group of male perpetrators, who were also survivors, about his abuse and its impact. Some members of the group applauded his willingness to do this; others were very angry, feeling that he was being exploited and his presence would in some way condone the perpetrators' actions. This led to a heated debate among all members, with very strong feelings being expressed on both sides.

Members' opinions on this matter were definite and largely intractable, and successful resolution involved helping members to see they could agree to disagree on the matter. For most, this was a new and novel approach to conflict resolution. As Jennifer commented, "The only thing I know about getting angry is that someone always gets hurt." Helping members to develop a respect and tolerance for their differing views on this issue was extremely therapeutic and instructive, and was, for most, a completely novel way of handling disagreement.

Members' Disappointment in Sally

In the two sessions following a particularly intense and painful one, all members attended except Sally. She did not contact anyone in the group, and the therapist was unable to reach her by phone. Finally contacted, Sally revealed to the therapist that the last group she had attended had "scared her to death, it was so tough." The therapist conveyed understanding, but urged Sally's return.

But Sally would only commit to coming for one more session. The therapist warned her that while members were concerned about her and would be glad to see her, she might also expect them to be angry with her. Sally said she understood and agreed to return once more.

In the next session, Sally explained her reasons for staying away and her concerns about continuing with the group. When asked for members' reactions, most commented that they were relieved to see her back. No one acknowledged feeling angry. "Now that Sally is back," the therapist explained, "it may be hard to get angry with her face to face. However, I sensed some of you were angry with her for leaving, and I just don't think that anger will go away without talking about it."

Reluctantly, two members of the group were able to express their disappointment with Sally and their anger with her for abandoning them. Another member affirmed these reactions, adding that he was angry at Sally because he wanted to see Sally "keep getting better, and quitting won't help with that."

With support, Sally was able to respond to members' concerns, ultimately saying, "I guess I let you down, as well as myself. To be honest, I really never thought that my leaving would make that much of a difference to you."

It was important for members to convey to Sally their disappointment and anger, and crucial for her to hear these sentiments and accept responsibility for the consequences of her actions. While Sally's fears about continuing were understandable, members' anger at her was also justified. Until this resentment was articulated and dealt with, it would have been impossible for the group to have proceeded with its work. Resolving this issue *was* important work for the group as everyone learned that they could survive the expression of anger directed toward another member.

Dealing with Connectedness

The group's focus on its immediate experiences does not just include managing conflict. As members' sense of connectedness with each other grows, so do their feelings of affection and positive regard. These feelings are equally discomforting to survivors. "I don't know that I even know what love is," said one member. "I know that whenever I have felt good about someone, I usually got hurt. I've learned to keep my distance. I also have to admit that I just don't feel worthy of anyone's affection."

Members Reach Out to George

In a particularly poignant moment in one group, George confided a conversation he had with his mother where he revealed thoughts of suicide. Her response, George said, was to offer to return his handgun to him. He was angry and extremely hurt, and members easily identified with and supported him. Much more difficult for members was to communicate caring for him, to tell him they did not want him to die because they would miss him.

The therapist had to work very hard to get members to share these feelings, which were clearly present, but difficult to articulate. In processing this with the group, one female member said, "You know, it's weird because I really do like George, and I feel so badly for him, and I really would miss him if he was gone, but I can't seem to tell him. It's like I'm so afraid of what he will do if he knows how I feel. It makes me feel so exposed."

Another female member, with tears in her eyes, finally said, "George, you seem like a lost little kid. When you talk there are times when I just want to hold you and tell you it will be all right. I really do like you and I really would miss you a lot if you weren't around."

This was a powerful moment in the life of this group. George received much-needed support and understanding, and members were able to start expressing feelings of affection for him and each other.

Group Self-Evaluation

It is important for members to feel a sense of responsibility and ownership toward the group. This leads to a sense of self-efficacy among members. It also enhances an understanding of their own behavior and the impact it has on others, and leads to greater sense of control. The therapist facilitates this perspective from the earliest sessions through the sessional review and eliciting members' feedback.

Increasingly, members need be able to take over the task of processing how they are doing, both individually and as a group. With adequate assistance, encouragement, and guidance in the early sessions from the therapist, members develop the ability to assess their progress as a group, identify important group themes and dynamics, and they become better able to identify and process these issues as they occur.

Some members become quite skillful at monitoring reactions of themselves and other individuals in the group, and assessing the group's overall focus. As the weeks progress, it is advisable for the therapist to refrain from making interpretations until others in the group have had the opportunity to do so. Process comments from members have a much greater impact, both on the group as a whole and on the individual members.

Jennifer and Denise Comment on the Group's Resistance

Two days before Thanksgiving, in the tenth group session, there was a great deal of idle chatter and jumping from subject to subject. After several attempts were made at focusing the group, Jennifer said to the therapist, "I see what you're trying to do. We really are all over the place tonight aren't we? We just don't want to talk about anything serious, I think. Holidays are rough, at least for me. Now more than ever is when I feel so alone and I realize how much I lost by never having a family. I'll bet I'm not alone. I'll bet that's the problem with us tonight. We just don't want to talk about our loneliness."

Several members of the group laughed nervously and agreed. Carol said, "Right. I've already shut down. I'm on automatic pilot from now through the middle of January. My defenses are up, for sure. I really can't afford to have the group get to me too much. Somehow I've got to get through the holiday." This sentiment was echoed by several others in the group.

An animated discussion followed about how members were having a hard time focusing on anything in group, and the protective function this served. Finally, Denise said, "Okay guys, enough is enough! The more we talk about how tough it is to talk about this stuff, the less we talk about what really matters! We've just got to start to deal with how lonely we are and how much we want to be part of a real family."

A number of the members had been in the preceding survivors' group, and this group's maturity, experience, and comfort level was evident. The most important observations about the way the group was working came from the members. Denise's assertion was particularly astute—the more the members focused on how hard it was talk about painful issues associated with the holiday, the more they avoided the discussion. With little assistance, the members processed and overcame their reluctance to focus on significant issues. Underscoring the importance of the refraining therapist, it was far more powerful and therapeutic for direction to come from the group, particularly when members have been together for a relatively long time.

Studies of the Here and Now in Group Therapy

Few studies have specifically and directly examined the impact of working in the here and now in therapy groups, despite the importance of this technique in group therapy. Findings of the few studies that exist are fairly consistent. Results suggest that insights provided by the group therapist to help members understand their behavior and identify ways to change are related to positive therapeutic outcomes. Such insights are most effective if they are linked to members' experiences in the session; the more abstract the interpretations, the less helpful they appear to be. Further, interpretative comments appear to be most beneficial if they occur after the group has achieved a certain level of cohesiveness. With respect to survivors specifically, one study has explored the relative merits of process-oriented groups and those that rely upon a structured format with an agenda for women. Women who were in the process group were particularly likely to evidence improvement in social functioning.*

FREQUENT LAUGHTER AND OTHER TENSION-RELIEVING BEHAVIOR

As the therapist was leaving after one group session, another therapist working a different part of the building commented, "Gee, you must have all had a good time in there! There sure was a lot of carrying on!" While this individual had not heard specific comments, what she did hear from time to time was loud, hearty laughter. Puzzled and clearly confused, she wondered, "How could a group of survivors possibly be having fun? Are they really working?"

Although they laughed frequently, the members were not having fun. A therapy group for survivors has numerous intense moments filled with despair, extraordinary sadness, and overwhelming rage, which at times, are difficult for members to endure. Laughter becomes a powerful, effective tool for coping with the group's intensity.

Silly jokes are common, as are "sick" jokes — morbid references to the abuse and other serious issues. This joking and laughter are not directed at any one member but reflect a phenomenon in which most or all members participate. Serving a much-needed and valuable purpose, laughing helps alleviate and dissipate some of the tension created by the group's focus on difficult issues. The group's ability to tackle painful subjects

---

See, for example: Abramovitz and Jackson 1974; Roback 1972; Whitney and Rose 1989; Flowers and Booarem 1989.

depends upon its ability to relieve the anxiety and stress that inevitably result.

As the group matures, members become better able to monitor this phenomenon and interpret its meaning. For example, several members, waiting for the group to start, were chatting, laughing, and generally acting silly. Ben commented, "I guess we're in for quite a group. If we're acting this way now, before it's even started, that must mean we have lots on our minds." Others laughed and concurred with this observation. This session followed a very intense one, in which several members were angry and where several others discussed serious problems they were having. The session did, indeed, prove to be a difficult one, and members picked up quickly where they had left off in the previous meeting.

Rarely does the therapist need to interrupt this behavior. When members are ready to get back to work, they will, with little or no help from the therapist. Of course, if the joking activity does not cease, and if members continue to avoid painful group work, the therapist would have to refocus the group.

The therapist may also have to assist some members in understanding this phenomenon. Some may assume that the laughter is malicious or directed at them, and it is helpful for the therapist to gauge the reactions of members and interpret the meaning of the laughter. Others in the group may be instrumental in helping the member understand that he or she has not been targeted for ridicule. Members become increasingly able to process their reactions with each other, better able to identify member discomfort associated with the joking, and respond to it appropriately.

Laughter and joking also reflect the growing camaraderie among group members. The group provides many members with their only opportunity to experience a sense of companionship with others. Members may congregate after group just to talk. As one member commented, "I just don't want to let go of the feeling that I have in group, of being accepted and connected to these guys. We don't even have to keep talking about the abuse and stuff, I just want to be with everybody."

To some extent, the laughter may be viewed as a naturally growing closeness among members. Whether it is a reflection of this phenomenon or an outlet for tension, it is a positive and inevitable feature of a therapy group for survivors.

RESENTMENT FOR THE THERAPIST

Unavoidable tension exists between members and the therapist. Although not unique to a group for survivors, several aspects of this resentment reflect survivors' distinctive treatment needs. Like many other clients, survivors struggle with strong feelings of bitterness towards individuals in positions of authority, reactions stemming from unresolved issues associated with parents, significant others, and the survivor's victimization. The group therapist clearly is in a position of authority, having responsibility for creating and running the group. Some member resentment may be viewed as a classic transference phenomenon.

Many survivors also have had previous experiences with therapists who were unsatisfactory, at best, and harmful, at worst. Unresolved anger regarding these experiences also may be directed at the group therapist.

The group therapist, at least in the early stages of the group, is primarily responsible for getting the group to work — getting the group to focus on and tackle the tough issues. This role, crucial as it is to a successful therapeutic experience, may further generate resentment among some members.

In instances where the therapist is not a survivor, members' resentment also may stem from bitterness towards individuals, generally, who were not sexually abused in childhood. To some extent this is an indication of the underlying anger at their abusers, but it also reflects their sense of outrage that they were victimized and others were not. As Tom said, "I just don't get it. Why me? Why not you? Am I so bad, so awful that I should have been raised by the perverts who were my parents? Why couldn't it have been you? Are you so much better than me?" As the only nonsurvivor in the group, the therapist commented, "There's no reason why you should have been abused and I shouldn't. It could have been me, but it wasn't. It was you, and that must make you angry as hell."

Dealing with Anger toward the Therapist

Regardless of the cause of anger at the therapist, it is important for members to articulate these feelings. Otherwise, the possibility exists that members will only go through the motions of working. If not resolved, members' feelings about the therapist may block their attempts to come to terms with their abuse, their feelings about it, and each other. It is important for survivors to know that they are likely to experience some anger at the therapist, and that it is acceptable for them to have these feelings and to express them.

Survivors need to learn how to deal with their anger and survive expressing it, especially when the anger is directed toward the therapist. The therapist's response to a member's anger can be extremely instructive. Such interaction paves the way for others to express their anger. The therapist has the responsibility of helping members directly articulate their concerns. If left to their own devices, members are unlikely to risk being honest in expressing feelings about the therapist. Angry feelings are threatening, and this is particularly true when they involve the therapist.

Expressing pent-up feelings often reawakens memories and fears associated with how members' anger was responded to in childhood. Group members may fear telling the therapist they are upset because they are afraid of the reaction. One member noted, "I know it sounds crazy, but I was afraid that you'd somehow hurt me, get back at me, if I said anything. I mean part of me knows you wouldn't. But another part, the little girl in me, was afraid you'd hurt me like my mother and father did."

The Therapist's Reaction to Anger

The therapist also must be able to tolerate the expression of anger directed at her or him. In most cases, members' anger is not warranted — the therapist has done nothing wrong. Often it is because the therapist has done something right that members' anger surfaces. While it is easy to understand why a therapist's reaction might be defensive, a more appropriate and helpful response would be for the therapist to assist members in expressing their anger and understand its source. If the therapist is uncomfortable, it is unlikely members' resentment and hostility will be dealt with openly and honestly. Not only must the therapist learn to tolerate angry reactions among members, she or he also must assist members to do the same. Resentment towards the therapist may be an ongoing issue for some members of the group and, in these cases, it is helpful to monitor the individual's reactions to the group, generally, and to the therapist, specifically. As resentment resurfaces, this should be pointed out and the member should be helped to talk about it.

Anger at the therapist is an unavoidable and standard aspect of group therapy. The effective group therapist is one who understands and, consequently, able to help both the individual member and the group as a whole to acknowledge and manage emotional reactions. Resentment towards the therapist is not just an individual-member issue, it is an issue for the group as a whole.

6
Ending the Group

Endings tend to be very difficult for members of a survivor's group. The group provides members with perhaps their only opportunity to feel connected to others, to experience fulfilling and rewarding relationships, and its cessation leads to strong feelings of sadness. While the group's work may have been difficult and painful, it also provided members with reassurance, support, and hope. The group's ending stimulates a resurgence of themes from earlier sessions, as members' anxieties and fears mount. While shifts in focus are subtle, indications point to members beginning to confront the group's ending.

Members work right to the very end, continuing to engage in frank discussions of sexuality, anger, and loss. As the group's end approaches members may try to cram everything in. As Sally said, "I realize that there are only three weeks left, and I feel there is still so much for me to work on. I knew when I started that everything wouldn't be resolved in 20 weeks, but somehow, now that it's really ending, I feel like there is so much I didn't do."

DENIAL OF THE GROUP'S ENDING

The painful prospect of ending manifests as avoidance and denial behavior. From the very beginning, the therapist reminds members how many weeks remain for the group to meet. Beginning in the tenth session — or the halfway point — the therapist should devote time in each session to the inevitable ending of the group and feelings members may have as a result.

It is likely that the therapist's comments will be met with silence. Survivors may be unable to talk directly about the eventual termination of the group. In earlier sessions the group's ending seems remote but, as the weeks progress, members become sad and fearful about the prospect of ending.

Sally Responds to the Therapist's Reminder

In the sixteenth week, the therapist reminded members that there would only be four more sessions and members seemed to want to forget that in another month they would no longer be together.

"You're right about that," Sally said. "I know we will end, although sometimes I think maybe something will happen and we'll still keep on. I know that sounds silly, but I just don't want to stop. I need this group and these people. I have no one. It's just me and my daughter. I really don't know what will happen to me if I don't have this group. So I just pretend that we'll just keep on meeting." Sally's comments typify members' sentiments on this issue, suggesting a strong need to deny the group's end.

The therapist has the obligation and challenging task of helping members prepare for and deal with the group's cessation. Despite all of the therapist's efforts, members' ability to focus directly on their feelings about ending may come late, sometimes not until the last session. While the therapist confronts and interprets members' denial, he or she may meet with only limited success. Sally's sentiments probably mirrored those of others in the group that "ending was really difficult and scary," but the therapist's encouragement of other members to discuss their feelings about ending was unsuccessful.

Even in the final session, members may avoid talking about the group's end. But the therapist can set the process of termination in motion by sharing her or his own feelings, by identifying each member's progress and strengths, as well as issues each needs to continue working on. The therapist must also provide members with a general sense of how they have worked together as a group, pointing out major themes and issues.

It is usually after the therapist has shared her or his own thoughts and feelings about the group's ending that members can begin doing the same. This is particularly true when it comes to expressing sadness. It is important for members to see their growth, as well as identify their next steps, to be able to say their farewells to each other and acknowledge openly how much the group has meant to them, and it is important for members to reflect on how they have worked together as a group.

Denial of ending is particularly likely to occur among survivors who have decided to join a subsequent group. These individuals are even more likely to avoid discussing termination, thinking, "What's the point? I'm coming back." When a group ends, members who arrange to keep in touch with each other, sharing phone numbers and addresses, often adopt the attitude, "We don't have to say goodbye because we're still going to see each other." In these situations, the therapist must continue to stress the importance and need for ending and assist members in realizing that the group — as they know it — will end.

ANGER AT THE THERAPIST

As the group approaches its end, a common reaction is members' anger toward the therapist. While members may be unable to talk directly about their feelings about ending, this dynamic suggests members are beginning the process of termination. To some extent, members blame the therapist for the group's ending. While this may be viewed as an extension of the more generalized anger at the therapist, the members are, in fact, correct — it is the therapist who limits the group to a specified number of sessions, and therefore it is the therapist's responsibility that the group is ending.

Since it is usually difficult for survivors to raise concerns on their own, the therapist needs to help members discuss their anger at him or her for the group's ending, acknowledging members' resentment and conveying that their anger is understandable.

Members can be expected to experience ambivalence about their anger toward the therapist but also some confusion surrounding their feelings about ending with each other. While most, if not all, members harbor some resentment toward the therapist about ending, they often can acknowledge they could use a break from the intense work of the group. On one hand they are sad and they may hold the therapist responsible for this sadness. On the other hand members may look forward to the group's ending with some sense of relief, desirous of some much-needed time off.

REGRESSION TO EARLIER THEMES

In the last stage of the group, regressive behavior is common and issues that surfaced in the earliest sessions emerge again. This reflects members' beginning attempts to come to terms with the group's termination.

Members' discussions begin to center on their fears and concerns about themselves and others. They again focus on their abuse and on other issues external to the group. They become less concerned with here-and-now interactions and more concerned with their lives outside the group. A few members may engage in regressive behavior, both inside and outside the group, reflecting their fears about going on alone without the group's support and encouragement. Feelings of isolation, inadequacy, and mistrust of others are rekindled. As was common in the earliest sessions of the group, members again idealize the group and attribute all of their progress to it. Members' attempts to prepare themselves for the loss of the group are apparent as less attention is centered on their dealings with each other and more is focused on problems that will concern them when the group ends.

For example, June told the group, "All of a sudden I began to think, I won't be seeing these folks again after two more weeks. That scares me. I wonder about whether I can manage. I realize that I still have all these problems in my life and suddenly they seem worse to me."

Not only are members likely to attribute all of their growth to the group, they are also prone to idealize their relationships with each other. Comments such as, "You guys are so special. There's no one else out there who can understand me like you do," are common. Pessimism is also expressed about experiencing satisfying relationships apart from the group. The mutuality developed among members, so crucial to the group's success, ultimately complicates their attempts to terminate with each other.

Members need help in articulating these anxieties and concerns, and understanding their significance. Members also require assistance in viewing the group realistically and in context. While members may experience an inevitable sadness about saying goodbye to those who have mattered to them, they also must recognize their hard work and the gains they have made.

It is only after members express their fears and anxieties that they can talk freely about their sadness and loss. This is not likely to occur until very late in the group, often in the last session. It is unlikely to take place at all if the therapist does not take a primary role in initiating the discussion.

INCREASE IN EXPRESSIONS OF SADNESS

While members may not yet be ready to talk about their sorrow regarding ending, this sentiment becomes evident in the group's increased focus on grief and sadness. In some cases, members disclose new information about losses they have suffered. More common is the tendency for members to reintroduce issues previously discussed, such as sadness regarding lost childhoods and innocence, or the death of significant individuals in their lives, metaphors for feelings about the group's end. Frank discussions of loss increase but its focus is centered on events and people outside the group's boundaries.

Members need assistance in seeing how the focus on loss is connected to their feelings about ending. It is likely they may still have a difficult time moving into an honest discussion of how they feel about ending with each other.

THE LAST SESSION

The group's work of saying goodbye and dealing with resultant sadness may not occur until the last session. The therapist can set this in motion by offering her or his own sentiments and observations about the group's termination. Beyond providing members with instructive insights into their current progress and possible future actions, the therapist's comments serve the important function of stimulating a similar discussion among the members. Although members may wait until the last session to talk about the group ending, when they finally do, the discussion is likely to be honest, intense, and full of both sorrow and hope.

Members may take turns, sequentially sharing their insights and observations about themselves and the group. In the last session, all members should be encouraged to participate, much like the first session where members introduce themselves.

Many members may express their feelings about ending with little help from the therapist. In a few cases, the therapist may need to assist a member in articulating and sharing feelings with the group. It is important for each member to see the progress made and to convey what the group has meant to her or him. For members who have difficulty either seeing the growth they have experienced or sharing their feelings about the group, the therapist's help is critical to their successful termination.

It is doubtful that any group for survivors can end without some or even all members feeling guilt about their actions or engaging in some second guessing. Sentiments such as, "What if . . . ," and "If only . . . ," reflect the underlying and long-standing feelings of self-blame and inadequacy plaguing survivors as a result of their victimization.

Open and honest discussion of mistakes in addressing and managing significant group issues and of what went right and what went wrong in the group, has the potential to minimize members' tendency toward self-reproach and may also be instructive. While discussion of ending helps members see the progress made and identify areas that continue to need work, it should also focus on an honest assessment of how they worked together. This clears the air, provides important feedback to the members, and is a valuable source of information for the therapist.

Throughout the group, members should be encouraged to examine the group process, themselves, and their relationships with each other. Even so, a thoroughly honest discussion of these issues as they emerge may be impossible to achieve. This is not only due to members' continued difficulties in talking frankly with each other, but also that an accurate perspective on important dynamics and themes requires a detachment simply not available to members as they immerse themselves in the work of the group. It may only be at the end, as the group finally winds down, that some important dynamics can be thoroughly and completely processed.

Addressing an Unresolved Issue

Much of the 20-session group had been dominated by George's concerns about his termination from individual therapy during the fifth group session. George's therapist felt he was a threat to her and George was preoccupied with this for the remainder of the group. His feelings ranged from rage at his therapist and the agency to an intense feeling of hurt and betrayal. Most of the time, however, his discussion in group centered on the ineptness of the agency and the therapist.

Initially, members were supportive and understanding of George's reactions to his termination. While they continued to support George, members increasingly felt frustrated by his inability to move beyond this occurrence, and their own inability to help him to do this. Two female members of the group, however, continued to support George, and expressed anger with the others for not standing by him.

Throughout the group, members' tensions and conflicts in responding to George grew. George's problems and the group's reactions to him were frequently addressed. Initially, the therapist introduced this discussion, but increasingly, the members were able to do this.

George's concerns did not inhibit the group's progress but because of them, a great deal of work took place around the management of anger, conflict, members' feelings of betrayal, and the fear that others would discover their true worthlessness. As the group ended, however, there appeared to be some unexpressed feelings about George. The therapist urged members to try to achieve some closure on this issue. One member expressed her anger toward the group for what she felt was their lack of concern for George's problem. One of the men replied, "Of course, I care. I'm really concerned about George. That's why I got so angry with him. He can't let those assholes at the agency make him feel crazy."

George remained quiet as members continued to debate their reactions. When George was asked to share his thoughts with the group, he expressed confusion, anger, and bitterness, claiming, "The group probably will be glad to get rid of me."

This led to a further intense discussion as members reacted, alternately, with guilt, understanding, anger, and frustration. The therapist told members that it was important to come to a sense of closure around this issue. "We all may have made some mistakes," the therapist said. "I'm not so sure that I handled this correctly either. We can all learn from what happened in this group." This led to a very productive and much-needed discussion of what the therapist, members, and George did correctly and what they could have done differently.

As this group was ending, the therapist was convinced that members had not worked through their feelings about this situation, nor had they been completely honest with her about her handling of it. For both reasons it was important to help the group to clear the air. As hard as it was for members to do this, the resulting discussion was instructive both to the members and the therapist. Based upon the members' comments, the therapist learned there were some things she could have done differently. While they may have disagreed in how they had reacted to George, members realized they all were concerned and cared about him. George continued to believe he was not welcome in the group, but he also began to understand that this reflected his own feelings of self-hatred, not the actual sentiments of the members.

While there was no actual solution to this group problem, everyone left feeling better about it, their sense of guilt and responsibility lessened. The therapist told the group, "We all learned from this, I think. We can either continue to beat our heads about what we did wrong, or we can vow to do things a little differently next time." Members appeared to agree with this view.

It was only after they had engaged in an extensive and frank discussion of this situation that members were able to say goodbye to each other — goodbyes that were tearful and heartfelt.

The Difficulty of Ending

Given the level of intense discussion and the strong sense of connectedness that develops, the group's ending is difficult for survivors. While members may be reluctant to explore feelings about ending directly, several group processes suggest members are dealing with the difficult task of saying goodbye.

The therapist needs to take the lead role in helping members articulate their concerns about termination, expressing her or his own feelings and thoughts, and use the emerging dynamics of the last sessions to reflect the group's concern with ending. A discussion of ending should include more than just the expression of sorrow and sadness. Although this is clearly important, members must also be helped to reflect honestly on their work together — not as a new activity, but a culminating one.

Ideally, all members leave the group with an enhanced sense of self-worth, a greater understanding of themselves and their victimization, and decreased feelings of isolation. Members should depart with increased feelings of comfort in interpersonal relationships, particularly involving the opposite sex. As has been argued throughout this book, these outcomes are dependent upon the therapist's ability to create a group in which honest discussion of the past and, increasingly, the immediate present has been the norm.

While endings are difficult for most groups, these are especially difficult for survivors, given their social isolation.

The experience of feeling connected to and accepted by others is very new and rewarding for survivors. The group's ending will also end — for many members — the only meaningful, satisfying relationships they have ever known. Sorrow around ending renews members' feelings of grief and sadness concerning their abuse.

A therapy group for survivors is a challenging and emotionally demanding endeavor, both for the participants and for the therapist. Its essential value lies in its ability to provide members with much needed validation and affirmation, a safe environment to explore their reactions to their abuse and to each other, the opportunity for members to experience intimacy and connectedness to others, and to leave with a sense of direction and optimism about their future.

Selected Bibliography

Abramovitz, Stephen, and Carolyn Jackson. "Comparative Effectiveness of There and Then Versus Here and Now Therapist Interpretations in Group Psychotherapy." *Journal of Counseling Psychology* 21 (1974): 288-93.

Alexander, Pamela, Robert Niemeyer, and Victoria Follette. "Group Therapy for Women Sexually Abused as Children: A Controlled Study and Investigation of Individual Differences." *Journal of Interpersonal Violence* 6 (1991): 218-31.

Alexander, Pamela, Robert Niemeyer, Victoria Follette, and Marlin Moore. "A Comparison of Group Treatment of Women Sexually Abused as Children." *Journal of Consulting and Clinical Psychology* 57 (1989): 479-83.

Alter-Reid, Karen, Margaret Gibbs, Juliana Lachenmeyer, Janet Sigal, and Neil Massoth. "Sexual Abuse of Children: A Review of the Empirical Findings." *Clinical Psychology Review* 6 (1986): 249-66.

American Medical Association. "Council Report: Scientific Status of Refreshing Recollection by the Use of Hypnosis." *Journal of the American Medical Association* 253 (1985): 1918-23.

Antonuccio, David, Cheryl Davis, Peter Lewinsohn, and Julia Breckenridge. "Therapist Variables Related to Cohesiveness in Group Treatment for Depression." *Small Group Behavior* 18 (1987): 557-64.

Apolinsky, Sandra, and S. Allen Wilcoxon. "Adult survivors of Childhood Sexual Victimization." *Family Therapy* 18 (1991): 37-45.

Aries, Elizabeth. "Interactional Patterns and Themes of Male, Female, and Mixed Groups." *Small Group Behavior* 7 (1976): 7-18.

Axelroth, Elie. "Retrospective Incest Group Therapy for University Women." *Journal of College Student Psychotherapy* 5 (1991): 81-100.

Barlow, Sally, William Hansen, Addie Fuhriman, and Robert Finley. "Leader Communication Style: Effect on Members of Small Groups." *Small Group Behavior* 13 (1982): 518-31.

Beasley, Lynda, and John Childers. "Group Counseling for Heterosexual, Interpersonal Skills." *Journal of Specialists in Groupwork* (November 1985): 192-97.

Bell, William, John Charping, and Jean Streaker. "Client Perceptions of the Effectiveness of Divorce Adjustment Groups." In *Advances in Groupwork Research,* edited by Sheldon Rose and Aaron Brower, 9-32. New York: Haworth Press, 1989.

Bonney, Warren, Donald Randall, and J. Diane Cleveland. "An Analysis of Client-Perceived Curative Factors in a Therapy Group of Former Incest Victims." *Small Group Behavior* 17 (1986): 303-21.

Bostwick, Gerald. " 'Where's Mary?' A review of the Group Dropout Literature." *Social Work with Groups* 10 (1987): 117-32.

Briere, John, and Jon R. Conte. "Self-Reported Amnesia for Abuse in Adults Molested as Children." *Journal of Traumatic Stress* 6 (1993): 21-31.

Briere, John, and Marsha Runtz. "Symptomatology Associated with Prior Sexual Abuse in a Non-Clinical Sample." Paper presented at the annual meeting of the American Psychological Association, Los Angeles, 1985.

————. "Symptomatology Associated with Childhood Sexual Victimization in a Non-Clinical Adult Sample." *Child Abuse and Neglect* 12 (1988): 51-59.

Briere, John, D. Evans, Marsha Runtz, and T. Wall. "Symptomatology in Men who Were Molested as Children: A Comparison Study." *American Journal of Orthopsychiatry* 58 (1988): 457-61.

Budman, Simon, and Annette Demby. "Short-Term Group Psychotherapy." In *Comprehensive Group Psychotherapy*, edited by Harold Kaplan and Benjamin Sadock, 138-44. Baltimore: Williams and Wilkins, 1983.

Budman, Simon, Annette Demby, Michael Feldstein, and Morris Gold. "The Effects of Time-Limited Group Psychotherapy: A Controlled Study." *International Journal of Group Psychotherapy* 34 (1985): 587-603.

Budman, Simon, Annette Demby, Jose Redondo, Marian Hannon, Michael Feldstein, and Jeffrey Ring. "Comparative Outcome in Time-Limited Individual and Group Psychotherapy." *International Journal of Group Psychotherapy* 38 (1988): 63-85.

Budman, Simon, Stephen Soldz, Annette Demby, Michael Feldstein, Tamar Springer, and Michael Davis. "Cohesion,

Alliance, and Outcome in Group Psychotherapy."
Psychiatry 52 (1989): 339-50.

Burden, Dianne, and Naomi Gottleib. "Women's Socialization
and Feminist Groups." In *Women's Therapy Groups,* edited
by Claire Brody. New York: Springer, 1987.

Burlingame, Gary, and Addie Fuhriman. "Time-Limited Group
Therapy." *The Counseling Psychologist* 18 (1990): 93-118.

Carlock, Charlene, and Patricia Martin. "Sex Composition and
the Intensive Group Experience." *Social Work* 22 (1977):
27-32.

Ceci, Stephen J., and M. Bruck. "Child Witnesses: Translating
Research into Policy." *Social Policy Report: Society for
Research in Child Development* 7 (1993): 1-30.

Cole, C., and E. Barney. "Safeguards and the Therapeutic
Window: A Group Treatment Strategy for Adult Incest
Survivors." *American Journal of Orthopsychiatry* 57
(1987): 601-09.

Colson, D., and L. Horwitz. "Research in Group
Psychotherapy." In *Comprehensive Group Psychotherapy,*
edited by Harold Kaplan and Benjamin Sadock, 304-11.
Baltimore: Williams and Wilkens, 1983.

Connelly, J., W. Piper, F. DeCarufel, and E. Debbane.
"Premature Termination in Group Psychotherapy:
Pre-Therapy and Early Therapy Predictors." *International
Journal of Group Psychotherapy* 36 (1986): 145-52.

Dies, Robert. "Clinical Implications of Research on Leadership
in Short-Term Group Psychotherapy." In *Advances in
Group Psychotherapy,* edited by Robert Dies and K. Roy

MacKenzie, 27-78. New York: International University Press, 1983.

Dies, Robert, and Lauren Cohen. "Content Considerations in Group Therapist Self-Disclosures." *International Journal of Group Psychotherapy* 26 (1976): 71-83.

Drum, David. "Reaction: Group Therapy Review." *Counseling Psychologist* 18 (1990): 131-38.

Edwards, Patrick, and Mary Ann Donaldson. "Assessment of Symptoms in Adult Survivors of Incest: A Factor Analytic Study of the Responses to Childhood Incest Questionnaire." *Child Abuse and Neglect* 13 (1989): 101-10.

Feldman-Summers, Shirley, and Kenneth Pope. "The Experience of 'Forgetting' Childhood Abuse: A National Survey of Psychologists." *Journal of Consulting and Clinical Psychology* 62 (1994): 636-39.

Feinauer, Leslie. "Comparison of Long-Term Effects of Child Abuse by Type of Abuse and by Relationship of the Offender to the Victim." *American Journal of Family Therapy* 17 (1989): 48-56.

————. "Relationship of Long-Term Effects of Childhood Sexual Abuse to the Identity of the Offender: Family, Friend, or Stranger." *Women and Therapy* 7 (1988): 89-107.

Finkelhor, David. "Early and Long-Term Effects of Child Sexual Abuse: An Update." *Professional Psychology: Research and Practice* 21 (1990): 325-30.

————. "The Trauma of Child Sexual Abuse: Two Models." *Journal of Interpersonal Violence* 2 (1987): 348-66.

Finkelhor, David, and Angela Browne. "The Traumatic Effects of Child Sexual Abuse: A Conceptualization." *Journal of Orthopsychiatry* 55 (1985): 530-41.

Flowers, John, and Curtis Booarem. "Four Studies toward an Empirical Foundation for Group Therapy." In *Advances in Groupwork Research,* edited by Shiela Rose and Aaron Brower, 105-21. New York: Haworth Press, 1989.

Follette, Victoria, Pamela Alexander, and William Follette. "Individual Predictors of Outcome in Group Treatment for Incest Survivors." *Journal of Consulting and Clinical Psychology* 59 (1991): 150-55.

Freeman-Longo, Robert. "The Impact of Sexual Abuse on Males." *Child Abuse and Neglect* 10 (1986): 411-14.

Fromuth, Mary, and Barry Burkhart. "Long-Term Psychological Correlates of Childhood Sexual Abuse." *Child Abuse and Neglect* 13 (1989): 533-42.

Gitterman, Alex, and Lawrence Shulman. "The Life Model, Mutual Aid, and the Mediating Function." In *Mutual Aid and the Life Cycle,* edited by Alex Gitterman and Lawrence Shulman, 3-22. Itasca, Ill: F.E. Peacock, 1986.

Gordon, Michael. "Males and Females as Victims of Childhood Sexual Abuse: An Examination of the Gender Effect." *Journal of Family Violence* 5 (1990): 321-32.

Greenwald, Evan, and Harold Leitenberg. "Post-Traumatic Stress Disorder in a Non-Clinical and Non-Student Sample of Adult Women Sexually Abused in Childhood." *Journal of Interpersonal Violence* 5 (1990): 217-29.

Herman, Judith, and Emily Schatzow. "Recovery and Verification of Memories of Childhood Sexual Trauma." *Psychoanalytic Quarterly* 4 (1987): 1-14.

Hilkey, James, Cynthia Wilhelm, and Arthur Horne. "Comparative Effectiveness of Videotape Pretraining Versus No Pretraining on Selected Process and Outcome Variables in Group Therapy." *Psychological Rep* 50 (1982): 1151-59.

Horenstein, David, and B. Kent Houston. "The Expectation-Reality Discrepancy and Premature Termination from Psychotherapy." *Journal of Clinical Psychology* 32 (1976): 373-78.

Hunter, John. "A Comparison of the Psychosocial Maladjustment of Adult Males and Females Sexually Abused in Childhood." *Journal of Interpersonal Violence* 6 (1991): 205-17.

Jacobs, M., O. Trick, and D. Withersty. "Pretraining Psychiatric Inpatients for Participation in Group Psychotherapy." *Psychotherapy: Theory, Research, and Practice* 13 (1976): 361-67.

Kelly-Garnett, Marcy. "Group Treatment of Sexual Abuse." *Journal of Reality Therapy* 8 (1989): 62-68.

Kiser, Laurel, Jerry Heston, Pamela Millsap, and David Pruitt. "Physical and Sexual Abuse in Childhood: Relationship with Post-Traumatic Stress Disorder." *Journal of the American Academy of Child Adolescent Psychiatrists* 30 (1991): 776-82.

Klein, R., and R. Carroll. "Patient Characteristics and Attendance Patterns in Outpatient Group Psychotherapy."

International Journal of Group Psychotherapy 36 (1986): 115-32.

Lazerson, Judith. "Feminism and Group Psychotherapy: An Ethical Responsibility." *International Journal of Group Psychotherapy* 42 (1992): 523-46.

Liberman, R. "Reinforcement of Cohesiveness in Group Therapy: Behavioral and Personality Changer." In *Group Psychotherapy Research: Commentaries and Selected Readings,* edited by Howard Roback, Stephen Abramovitz, and Donald Strasberg, 181-91. New York: Robert Krieger Publishing, 1979.

Loftus, Elizabeth. "The Reality of Repressed Memories." *American Psychologist* 48 (1993): 518-37.

MacKenzie, K. Roy, and Volker Tschuschke. "Relatedness, Groupwork, and Outcome in Long-Term Inpatient Psychotherapy Groups." *Journal of Psychotherapy Practice and Research* 2 (1993): 147-56.

Mackey, Theresa, Sylvia Hacker, Lisa Weissfeld, and Nancy Ambrose. "Comparative Effects of Sexual Assault on Sexual Functioning of Child Sexual Abuse Survivors and Others." *Issues in Mental Health Nursing* 12 (1991): 89-112.

Mayer, Adele. *Repressed Memories of Sexual Abuse.* Holmes Beach, FL: Learning Publications, 1995.

McEvoy, Maureen. "Repairing Personal Boundaries: Group Therapy with Survivors of Sexual Abuse." In *Healing Voices: Feminist Approaches to Therapy with Women,* edited by Toni Laidlaw and Cheryl Malmo, 29-44. San Francisco: Jossey-Bass, 1990.

McEvoy, Maureen and L. Minuk. "Repairing Personal Boundaries: Group Therapy with Survivors of Sexual Abuse." In *Healing Voices: Feminist Approaches to Therapy with Women,* edited by T. Laidlaw and C. Malmo, 29-44. San Francisco: Jossey-Bass, 1990.

Melnick, Joseph, and Martha Woods. "Analysis of Group Composition Research and Theory for Psychotherapeutic and Growth-Oriented Groups." *Journal of Applied Behavioral Science* 12 (1976): 493-511.

Morran, D. Keith, Rex Stockton, and Linda Bond. "Delivery of Positive and Corrective Feedback in Counseling Groups." *Journal of Counseling Psychology* 38 (1991): 410-14.

Morrison, James, Judith Libow, Frederick Smith, and Robert Becker. "Comparative Group Therapist Style on Client Problem Resolution." *Journal of Clinical Psychology* 34 (1978): 186-87.

Myers, Michael. "Men Sexually Assaulted as Adults and Sexually Abused as Boys." *Archives of Sexual Behavior* 18 (1989): 203-15.

Neimeyer, Robert, Stephanie Harter, and Pamela Alexander. "Group Perceptions as Predictors of Outcome in the Treatment of Incest Survivors." *Psychotherapy Research* 1 (1991): 148-58.

Palmer, Robert, Rhoda Oppenheimer, A. Dignon, and D. Chaloner. "Childhood Sexual Experiences with Adults Reported by Women with Eating Disorders." *British Journal of Psychiatry* 156 (1990): 699-703.

Piper, William, and Ellen Perrault. "Pretherapy Preparation for Group Members." *International Journal of Group Psychotherapy* 39 (1989): 17-34.

Putnam, Frank, Juliet Guroff, and Edward Silberman. "The Clinical Phenomenology of Multiple Personality Disorder: A Review of 100 Recent Cases." *Journal of Clinical Psychiatry* 47 (1986): 285-93.

Reed, Beth Glover. "Gender Issues in Training Group Leaders." *Journal of Specialists in Group Work* 6 (1981): 161-70.

Roback, Howard. "Experimental Comparison of Outcomes in Insight- and Non-Insight-Oriented Therapy Groups." *Journal of Consulting and Clinical Psychology* 38 (1972): 411-71.

Roback, Howard, and Maribeth Smith. "Patient Attrition in Dynamically Oriented Treatment Groups." *American Journal of Psychiatry* 144 (1987): 426-31.

Russell, Diana, Rachel Schurman, and Karen Trocki. "The Long-Term Effects of Incestuous Abuse: A Comparison of Afro-American and White American Victims." In *Lasting Effects of Child Sexual Abuse*, edited by Gail Wyatt and Gloria J. Powell, 119-34. Newbury Park, CA: Sage, 1988.

Salter, Anna. *Transforming Trauma: A Guide to Understanding and Treating Adult Survivors of Child Sexual Abuse.* Thousand Oaks, CA: Sage Publications, 1995.

Sgroi, Suzanne. *Handbook of Clinical Intervention in Child Sexual Abuse.* Lexington, MA: D.C. Heath, 1982.

————. "Healing Together: Peer Group Therapy for Adult Survivors of Child Sexual Abuse." In *Vulnerable Populations: Sexual Abuse Treatment for Children, Adult Survivors, Offenders, and Persons with Mental Retardation,* Vol. 2, edited by Suzanne Sgroi, 131-66. Lexington, MA: D.C. Heath, 1989.

Shulman, Lawrence. *The Skills of Helping Individuals, Families, and Groups.* Itasca, Ill: F.E. Peacock, 1992.

Stein, Judith, Jacqueline Golding, Judith Siegal, M. Audrey Burnham, and Susan Sorenson. "Long-Term Sequelae of Child Sexual Abuse: The Los Angeles Epidemiologic Cachement Area Study." In *Lasting Effects of Child Sexual Abuse,* edited by Gail Wyatt and Gloria J. Powel, 135-54. Newbury Park, CA: Sage, 1988.

Stockton, Rex, D. Keith Morran, and Patricia Velkoff. "Leadership of Therapeutic Small Groups." *Journal of Group Psychotherapy, Psychodrama, and Sociometry* 39 (1986): 157-65.

Terr, Lenore. *Too Scared to Cry: How Trauma Affects Children . . . and Ultimately Us All.* New York: Basic Books, 1990.

Tolman, Richard, and Gauri Bhosley. "A Comparison of Two Types of Pre-Group Preparation for Men who Batter." *Journal of Social Service Res* 13 (1989): 33-43.

Urquiza, Anthony, and C. Crowley. "Sex Differences in the Survivors of Childhood Sexual Abuse." Paper presented at the Fourth Conference on the Sexual Victimization of Children, New Orleans, LA, 1986.

Vander Mey, Brenda. "The Sexual Victimization of Male Children: A Review of Previous Research." *Child Abuse and Neglect* 12 (1988): 61-72.

Williams, L. "Adult Memories of Childhood Abuse: Preliminary Findings from a Longitudinal Study." *APSAC Advisor* 5 (1992): 19-22.

Wheeler, Inese, Kathleen O'Malley, Michael Waldo, James Murphy, and Cheryl Blank. "Participants' Perceptions of Therapeutic Factors in Groups for Incest Survivors." *Journal of Specialists in Groupwork* 17 (1992): 89-95.

Whitney, Dale, and Sheldon Rose. "The Effect of Process and Structured Content on Outcome in Stress Management Groups." In *Advances in Groupwork Research,* edited by Sheldon Rose and Aaron Brower, 89-104. New York: Haworth Press, 1989.

Wright, F., P. Burski, and N. Smith. "The Implications of Leader Transparency for the Dynamics of Short-Term Process." *Group* 2 (1978): 210-19.

Wyatt, Gail, and M. Ray Mickey. "Ameliorating the Effects of Child Sexual Abuse: An Exploratory Study of Support by Parents and Others." *Journal of Interpersonal Violence* 2 (1987): 403-14.

Yalom, Irvin. *The Theory and Practice of Group Psychotherapy.* New York: Basic Books, 1985.

Yalom, Irvin, P. Houts, S. Zimerberg, and K. Rand. "Predictions of Improvement in Group Therapy: An Exploratory Study." In *Group Psychotherapy Research: Commentaries and Selected Readings,* edited by H. Roback,

S. Abramovitz, and D. Strasberg, 129-37. New York: Robert Krieger Publishing, 1979.

Young, Walter, Roberta Sachs, Bennett Braun, and Ruth Watkins. "Patients Reporting Ritual Abuse in Childhood: A Clinical Syndrome." *Child Abuse and Neglect* 15 (1991): 181-89.